THE BEST OF WRITERS' MONTHLY

Other Allison & Busby Writers' Guides:

How to Write Stories for Magazines by Donna Baker
How to Produce a Play by Doris M. Day
The Craft of Novel-Writing by Dianne Doubtfire
Writing for Radio by Colin Haydn Evans
How to Publish Your Poetry by Peter Finch
How to Publish Yourself by Peter Finch
How to Write a Play by Dilys Gater
The Craft of TV Copywriting by John Harding
How to Write for Children by Tessa Krailing
Dear Author . . . by Michael Legat
How to Write Historical Novels by Michael Legat
Writing Step by Step by Jean Saunders
The Craft of Writing Romance by Jean Saunders
The Craft of Writing TV Comedy by Lew Schwarz
The Craft of Writing Articles by Gordon Wells
The Magazine Writer's Handbook by Gordon Wells
The Book Writer's Handbook by Gordon Wells
Writers' Questions Answered by Gordon Wells
The Craft of Effective Letter Writing by Gordon Wells
Photography for Article-Writers by Gordon Wells
How to Write for Teenagers by David Silwyn Williams

THE BEST OF WRITERS' MONTHLY

Edited by

Gordon Wells
(in consultation with the Editor of *Writers' Monthly*)

ALLISON & BUSBY

First published in Great Britain in 1992 by
Allison & Busby
An imprint of Virgin Publishing Ltd
338 Ladbroke Grove
London W10 5AH

Editorial content copyright © Gordon Wells 1992
Individual contributions copyright © indicated authors/
WM publication dates

This book is sold subject to the condition that it shall not, by way of trade or otherwise, be lent, resold, hired out or otherwise circulated without the publisher's prior written consent in any form of binding or cover other than that in which it is published and without a similar condition including this condition being imposed upon the subsequent purchaser.

ISBN 0 7490 0084 8

Phototypeset in Times by Intype, London

Printed and bound in Great Britain by
Mackays of Chatham Ltd, Lordswood, Kent.

CONTENTS

Introduction 7

1 WRITING FICTION 9

Write a Novel in Six Months 11
   Dilys Gater (*WM* August 1988)
A Chapter on Cliff-Hangers 17
   Angela Wells (*WM* August 1989)
The Brand New Reader 20
   Anne Forsyth (*WM* October 1990)
What's in a Name? 25
   Bill Bradley (*WM* April 1990)
Tips for Writing Short Stories 30
   Syd Bounds (*WM* March 1989)

2 WRITING NON-FICTION 33

Finding Ideas 35
   Alison Bremner (*WM* November 1988)
Twenty Tips for Article Writers 38
   Marian Hardless (*WM* June 1988)
Sidebars That Sell 42
   Raymond Palmer (*WM* July 1989)
Selling a Non-Fiction Book 46
   Gordon Wells (*WM* October 1989)
Tackling the Textbook 52
   Derek Gregory (*WM* May 1989)

3 WRITING DRAMA – AND POETRY 59

Writing for Amateur Theatre 61
   Mary Rensten interviews David Campton
   (*WM* August 1988)

Writing a Pantomime   67
   Jackie Short (*WM* September 1988)
Oh No She Didn't!   70
   Ann Stevens (*WM* December 1990)
Creating Landscapes in the Mind   74
   Bill Bradley (*WM* August 1989)
The Joke's on You   79
   Jim Eldridge (*WM* July 1989)
Getting a Book of Poems Published   85
   Glyn Maxwell (*WM* January 1989)

4 WRITING STYLE   91

Do You Mean That Literally?   92
   Jim McIntosh (*WM* July 1989)
Strictures on Structure   98
   Jim McIntosh (*WM* March 1989)

5 A WRITER'S LIFE AND BUSINESS   105

The Editor's Always Right!   107
   Martin Horan (*WM* February 1989)
Research for Writers   111
   Jim Rees (*WM* December 1988)
Marketing Matters   118
   Elizabeth Balfour (*WM* April 1990)
How to Market Your Books by Guest Speaking   123
   Brenda Courtie (*WM* September 1988)

INTRODUCTION

Books are books and articles are articles. There is a difference – and not just in the length. There are article subjects and there are book subjects.

Many topics which make excellent articles are not suitable for expansion into a book; many article topics are difficult to fit within the carefully planned structure of a full-length book. Article subjects seldom appear in books. They are written for magazines – and are published in magazines.

But magazines are ephemeral things. Maybe you keep 'em for a month or so – but then you throw them away (unless you're like me, and hoard every issue of your favourite magazine). And all those very interesting, very useful, articles are lost.

Or maybe you tear out the interesting articles to keep? And then forget where you put the tear-sheets. There has to be a better way.

There is. The answer is an anthology, a collection of useful articles brought together under a few loose headings to make a full-length book of reprints. And that's what this book is. An anthology of particularly useful articles about various aspects of writing – *the best* of the advice articles that have appeared in the last few years' issues of *Writers' Monthly*.

Writers' Monthly is an excellent, and now well-established, magazine for writers: it has something in it for every wordsmith – beginner or old hand alike. And many of the articles that have appeared in its pages are ones I have wanted to keep, to refer back to. Nearly all of the articles appearing in *Writers' Monthly* are by experts in their field. (The 'nearly all' qualification is necessary because sometimes there is an equally helpful article telling of the difficulties – and successes – of a beginner.)

Some of the articles in *Writers' Monthly* are of immediate, but not necessarily long-lasting, interest. Others though, are chock-full of timeless advice: hints and tips that will be as valid in the 21st century (not so far away now) as they are today.

With the cooperation and unstinted assistance of the Editors of *Writers' Monthly*, I have selected a bookful of these timeless articles on the writing business. You will not need to strain your memory to recall where you saw that article about writing sidebars – it's here; you will no longer need to riffle through your pile of back issues, searching for that article about getting a poetry book published – it's here; the article on cliff-hangers is here too. And so is the advice on how to start *your* novel – or your first pantomime.

How then is this collection, this potential rag-bag, of advice articles put together and organized? How else than by the different areas of writing interest: fiction, non-fiction, poetry and drama, general writing style, and the business of being a writer. There is something for everyone – and it is also strongly recommended that you delve into the advice offered in areas outside your normal ken. Who knows, you might have the makings of a poet . . . and not know it. (Sorry!)

The initial selection was mine. Throughout, I sought to maintain a balance between the different writing interests. Most of all, I looked for positive advice. I also looked for inspirational pieces that made me want to 'go and do likewise'. And I looked for the unusual. I found all of these.

My preliminary selection of articles was then reviewed by the Editor of *Writers' Monthly* – to whom I am most grateful. I accept the brickbats for any faults in the selection; she and her predecessors deserve all the bouquets for having selected the articles for publication in the first place.

Gordon Wells

1

WRITING FICTION

Everyone wants to write a novel. Somehow, you aren't really an *author* unless you've written a novel. To write a novel – or even a short story – requires the exercise of imagination. That is deemed *creative*.

Whether or not those sentiments are correct matters not. They are undoubtedly in the minds of many would-be writers. Beginning writers usually dream of writing 'the great novel', or – if they seek a supposedly easier approach – at least a short story. (I understand though, that a short story can often be more difficult to write than a novel.) And storytelling is an honourable trade.

So, this section of the book offers advice to the would-be writer of fiction. To start you off, there is a truly motivational article by Dilys Gater, 'Write a Novel in Six Months'. This takes the form of an assignment which you are invited to accept. Work to this strenuous timetable – and become a novelist. Dilys Gater is herself a published novelist and a teacher of writing. She knows what it takes.

The ability to keep the readers turning the pages, to hold them in *thrall*, is the mark of a true storyteller. And one of the tricks of the storytelling trade is to end each chapter with a cliff-hanger – to leave Pauline tied to the railway track as the train comes thundering round the bend. Romantic storyteller Angela Wells offers excellent advice on how to think up fresh Perils for Pauline, and keep the pages turning, in 'A Chapter on Cliff-Hangers'.

Also in this section of the book, children's writer Anne Forsyth looks at the responsibilities and problems of writing for 'The Brand New Reader'; all-rounder Bill Bradley asks, rhetorically, 'What's in a Name?' and points out the importance – and significance – of the names you ascribe to your places and characters; and prolific writer Syd Bounds gives several 'Tips for Writing Short Stories' – how to please both editors and readers.

In all, a well-rounded selection of hints and tips for fiction writers. Dive in. The water's warm.

Write a Novel in Six Months

Dilys Gater

Your Brief
You have been asked to write a novel of approximately 60,000 words about any aspect of relationships in contemporary society. Deadline: Six months from now.

Month One
Your novel will occupy roughly 170–180 pages of type double-spaced on A4 paper with one inch margins. If you want to write it in longhand, you will have to work out a rough estimate of the number of pages your handwriting will take up. In six months, these pages will be filled with the chapters of your novel.

If you want to force yourself to do a certain amount of work every day or week to get to the end, aim for roughly 10,000 words each month, or just over 2,000 words each week. On the other hand, there is no rule that you must work every day. Some people can write better if they concentrate for eight hours or all night once they get going, then leave it for several days. The choice is yours.

Advice: never try to write when you are too tired, upset or worried. Many writers can work better under pressure, but a tired and exhausted brain will be slow, and will not produce good work. Try to come to your novel when you are fresh and alert.

In Month One, you will write the *beginning* of your novel. Before you begin, you will want to consider the *style*, *pace*, *characters* and *plot*.

Style
Every person in the world has their own unique and individual style of writing. It is inherent in the way you think and put words and sentences together. You will not realise, possibly, that you have a style of your own. You will worry about making your novel 'literary' or 'original'. Forget such problems. They do not exist. All you will achieve if you consciously try to impose a 'literary'

or 'original' style onto the way you would normally write, is a false, stiff and unnatural narrative. Be yourself. Say what you want to say, in your own way. Without any effort at all on your part, your work will be original and – if you have a reasonable knowledge of English – there is no reason why it should not also read well. That is all you need to worry about.

Pace

The pace of a novel means the speed at which events happen in the story. If your plot is going to span 20 years, events must move quickly, and there will not be time for your characters to indulge in a deep self-analysis or complicated thoughts which might take them several pages to work out.

On the other hand, if you have decided that it is the happenings of one significant weekend which you are going to chronicle, the pace will be correspondingly slower, and you *can* describe small details, and explore the impressions and feelings and moods of your characters, in a leisurely manner.

Characters

There are various methods writers use to create their characters. Some collect pictures of faces from magazines, and stare at them until they see a face that gives them a character they are trying to find. Others use faces or figures they have glimpsed on a bus, or in the street, without knowing who the actual people were. Others take people they know and alter them a bit. You will find your own best way of creating characters.

When you begin your story, you are picking up the lives of your characters at a certain point in their relationships. Choose the point where your novel is going to start with care. Remember that things have happened to these people before Chapter One begins. You must bear in mind that they all have their own previous history, they have done things, experienced things, which have made them the characters they are.

Advice: always *show* character, not simply tell it. The colour of the heroine's eyes is less important than the fact that when she comes across an injured bird, she cares enough about it to pick it up and hold it in her hand until it recovers from its shock and flies away from her. Physical details are not always necessary, so don't pepper your sentences with them. The heroine of *Rebecca* was hardly described, and her name was never given, but she is grippingly real to the reader.

Plot
Real life has no plot, it is a series of incidents. Your novel must have a theme that will run through it and hold it together; it must tell some sort of story that has a beginning, middle and end. Anyone who writes up something from their own experience and says 'This really happened, so it must be good', has no knowledge of what a plot is.

It is an artificial framework, a series of minor conflicts and climaxes that culminate in some sort of resolution at the end of the story. You may not know exactly what you are going to include in your plot when you start the novel, and may not know just how the resolution will happen.

Often a plot springs as much as artistic work does, from the subconscious, and will shape itself as you go along. But you must have at least a vague idea of your ending, even if you're not sure of the details. And so, in Month One, you have thought of all these things, and you have started to write.

Months Two and Three
As you continue to work on your novel, beware of the two following traps:

1. Avoid the temptation to go back and re-read the early pages. You will end up either so convinced that they are awful that you lose all your confidence, or else you will think they are so wonderful you'll feel whatever you write next will be a let-down. Don't look back, keep moving forward.

2. Don't discuss your work with your wife, husband, or a friend, or you may 'talk out' the whole story and once you do this, you will lose it and never be able to write it down on paper. However excited you become as the work progresses, however thrilled that your characters are taking on decisions of their own, becoming real to you, that the plot is working out, try not to talk about what you are writing. Wait until you get to the end. It will be an effort, but try hard to keep your own counsel.

All that you write will come out of your own head and your own experience, but learn to be selective, to choose incidents carefully. If you come to a standstill, and feel you can't go on, write any sort of linking passage until your characters pick themselves up again and start to live once more.

It is surprising how what seemed to be a terrible obstacle can, when you look back on it, be eased over by rewriting just a few sentences. Once you get to the end, you will see the shape of the whole thing, and can clear up bits that were difficult to write at the time.

But KEEP GOING. For every novel that gets finished, there are thousands that are abandoned halfway. Yours isn't going to be one of those! You have a deadline to meet, remember?

Months Four and Five
The halfway mark of a novel is often where despair sets in and the writer gives up. The novelty of the early chapters will have worn off, you may even feel you are sick to death of your characters. The plot is getting very sticky, too, and you're sure you should have tackled the whole thing another way.

Many people are unaware that writing a novel is *hard work*. 60,000 words is a lot to write, and you also have to sustain your flagging enthusiasm over quite a long period of time.

But once you've passed the halfway mark, you can tell yourself that you're on the home stretch now. It's downhill all the way.

By this time, you should be becoming aware of how the novel is going to end, and you must be careful that you do not, in your eagerness and relief, anticipate the ending and so spoil it. Let the drama play itself out without a last desperate spurt to try and reach the ending quickly.

If you have kept a good grip on your plot as it unfolds, you should be able to plan the ending carefully so that the book reaches a climax, building up to it and carrying the reader with you.

Month Six
Strangely, one of the most difficult things for an inexperienced writer is to know when and where to end a novel. Once you have detailed the climax, and the story is told, it is just as much of a mistake to end the story too abruptly as it is to drag it out long after the last page should have been written.

Depending, of course, on your story, it is often a good idea to finish on an up-beat, perhaps an open question mark. Note the end of *Gone With The Wind* – 'Tomorrow is another day'. One story ends, another may be about to begin, but though your readers are dying to read it, your last sentence is written, your novel is finished.

'Oh, I wish it had gone on,' your readers sigh, closing the pages reluctantly. If you can leave your readers wanting more, yet at the same time, satisfied as well because your ending marked the final comments you had to make on the story you have just told, you will have really achieved something.

A certain amount of tidying up of loose ends will be necessary at the close of your novel, but beware long drawn-out explanations that are not needed. You may want to end on a comment one of the characters makes, but feel that this would not be right. There is nothing to stop you, so long as the comment is in character and not some sort of oratorical utterance to mark THE END. Remember that your characters are going to carry on with their lives after the story is finished. At least, that is the impression you want to leave with the reader.

And so, at last, that is it. You have finished. But – alas – there is still more work to be done on your 60,000 words. You'll probably feel so euphoric that you decide to celebrate your great achievement with champagne. I'm all for that. But the next day, put the manuscript away and don't look at it for at least a week. (Some people recommend six months!) Then get it out and read through it as clinically as possible.

Mistakes and errors will leap out and hit you on all sides. Correct your work, cut out unnecessary sentences or phrases, clarify if you think some point is obscure. Do all you can to improve it, but avoid another trap that many writers of first novels fall into at this stage. They enjoy revising their great opus so much that they can't stop tinkering with it. It's wonderful, of course, and isn't it fun to keep altering a word here and there, admiring the whole thing, thinking about how clever you've been to write it in the first place? *Do not do this.*

After re-reading and correcting, you'll probably need to have the manuscript freshly typed. If you can't face doing this yourself, have it done for you. And then let the novel go out into the world to meet its fate, whatever that is to be.

Send it to an editor. Submit it for publication. Once you've posted the package (if you want to become a professional writer of novels), forget about it and start thinking about the opening pages of . . . your SECOND book!

Dilys Gater has been a professional writer for 20 years. Her career covers broadcasting, journalism and writing full-length works of fiction and non-fiction. She has written over 50 books under six pseudonyms and been published all over the world. She has taught writing, and written numerous books and articles on 'how to write'.

A Chapter on Cliff-Hangers

Angela Wells

One of the questions I am most often asked when speaking to fellow writers at Writers' Circles is: 'How on earth do authors manage to get all their chapters roughly the same length?' Sometimes it's put another way: 'How in heaven do authors manage to finish each chapter at the right length and end on a cliff-hanger at the same time so that the reader is compelled to begin the next chapter without a break . . . and the next . . .?'

To be honest, I don't know how other writers cope with this problem, but I'm quite willing to tell you how I do.

When I first started writing I had a good idea of the storyline, notes of the main events on which the plot turned, an idea of approximately at which point in the book they should be introduced and (hopefully) a strong, happy-ever-after ending. I knew too that I was aiming for 50,000 to 55,000 words so that each chapter should contain about 5,000 words.

It should have been simple after that, shouldn't it? I can assure you it wasn't.

Schooled in the old-fashioned way I believed that, just as every sentence should have a subject, verb and object, so every chapter should have a logical beginning and end. The net result of this was that every one of my chapters began with someone getting up in the morning and ended with someone turning in for the night. And because my 'logical' events varied in length, some chapters had as little as 2,000 words whilst others had as many as 8,000. Clearly this wouldn't do. Not only were the chapters unwieldy, they were also ineffably boring.

At my wits' end I decided some dynamic thought was required. After a great deal of editing (consisting mainly of removing large chunks of purple prose soul-searching – yes, I know it makes you feel good to write it, but if you're interested in the popular markets avoid the temptation) I had managed to tell my story in the required 55,000 words. Right, I decided, what I needed was 11 chapters each of 5,000 words.

Ruthlessly, I divided my MS up into 11 equal piles of A4 and with the bravado of a matador facing a bull, knowing only one of us will emerge unscathed, I took a long hard look at what was before me. The result was both gratifying and surprising.

Not every arbitrary division was perfect. But in every case within one page of the arithmetically arrived at break there was a definite possibility of a chapter ending, and conversely a beginning.

Let me give you an example. Would you, as an unpublished writer striving for recognition think of ending your chapter in the middle of a conversation? Probably not. Certainly not if you'd undergone the kind of English tuition in which my convent school specialised. (See, no prepositions at the end of sentences either – habit dies hard!) You would be right to have reservations if the last line of your conversation was, for instance, *'Would you prefer to have a meringue or a chocolate eclair, Miranda?'*

However, supposing you end your chapter with something like:

'I've been waiting for this moment for a long time Miranda!' Robert seized her arms with steel fingers. 'You're not going to leave this room until you tell me the truth!'

The next chapter then begins: *Miranda closed her eyes against the threat she could read in Robert's cold, grey eyes, aware that her day of reckoning had arrived at last, and she must deliver the facts he wanted or be for ever damned in his eyes.*

Get the idea? It's all quite illogical – but very effective, especially if you're after generating the kind of tension and expectation that makes your reader go on turning the page.

After a while you'll probably find that you know subconsciously when you're reaching the wordage for which you're aiming, and the required 'peak' will come quite naturally off your pen, or WP.

'But suppose I have a time lapse in the narrative?' I'm sometimes asked. 'Shouldn't I begin a new period of action with a new chapter?'

This is slightly more difficult and probably depends on the length of the time lapse in relation to the total duration of the time within the scope of the novel. Comparatively small lapses, days, weeks, even a few months can be accommodated within the text by leaving a couple of blank lines, or centring three asterisks between paragraphs – whichever is preferred by the house style of your would-be publisher. Provided you let your reader know what's going on, you should have no problem.

She'd never felt more bored in her life, Miranda thought miserably, running her feather duster over the picture rail of the small bedroom. Three weeks since that last vivid encounter with Robert and she was still living in a kind of vacuum, her days filled with nothing more exciting than the usual household chores, including waiting in those interminably long queues at the fast check-out of the local supermarket.

'Oh', she gave a little shriek as the insistent beep-beep of the telephone downstairs in the hall pierced her lethargy, jarring her into action . . .

And we're off again.

No problem, is there!

A time lapse of three months or more and I think I would start a new chapter. Simply re-divide the existing MS into new uniform sections in front of the chapter in question.

Take a look at some of the books in your own library. I bet you find that the ones that have never left your hands until the last word has been read actually have chapter breaks your old English teacher would find most unorthodox.

And it works as a friend of mine will readily testify.

'I started reading your latest book in bed,' she said crossly, 'thinking I'd just read the first chapter before I settled down for the night. Two hours later I was still reading because every time I got to the end of a chapter the action hadn't finished. In the end my husband complained bitterly that the light was keeping him awake and I had to go and finish reading in the bathroom!'

One romance that obviously didn't start an amorous chain of events! But from our point of view, fellow writer, that's what it's all about. Isn't it!

Angela Wells writes contemporary romance novels. Her first was published by Mills & Boon in 1985 (after much editorial guidance); by early 1991 she had had a further twelve accepted by the same publisher. Her books have appeared in hardback, paperback and large print and have been translated into thirteen different languages.

The Brand New Reader

Anne Forsyth

Imagine the blueprint for the ideal reader. He or she is lively, very curious, always ready to be amused. This reader will write warmly appreciative letters to an author. 'I really laughed.' 'I enjoyed it so much, I read it to my dad – and he liked it too.'

There you are. My ideal reader is aged about seven, full of imagination and enthusiasm. That's why I write for five to eight year olds, and why I find it such a rewarding market.

In the trade, they're known as beginner readers. For the writer, it's a market that's growing. And with the recent publicity about children's reading, it's a market that promises to be with us for a long time.

Suppose a child has just learned to read. The next stage is reading a book – a real book – alone. With luck, the child attends a school where teachers care passionately about books. They want simple but enjoyable stories, easy to read, attractive to handle.

When I began writing for children, nine years ago, there were only a few well-established series for beginner readers. Now every children's publisher seems to have a list for the new reader: the series will have a catchy title, the books will be well illustrated with bright full colour covers, the covers laminated so that they are easy to keep clean.

The stories are short – about 2,500 or 3,000 words. There are pictures on each page so that the child's interest is captured. A whole double spread of print is daunting at this stage of reading. The use of lively pictures helps to ensure that the child turns the page to find out what happens next.

The content? Well, it varies. Animal stories are popular, so are ghost stories – and of course humour, lots of it.

So you want to write for this market? Not, please, because it's easy to toss off 2,500 words and you may have a few stories stuck in a drawer.

It's *not* an easy, ready-made market. There are lots of authors around, and publishers' standards are exacting.

I don't pretend to expertise, but here are a few hints I've picked up along the way.

For this market, as for any other, you have to do your homework, find out what publishers want, and test your material.

So where do you start? Not necessarily in your local bookshop. There are so many beginner readers series that your bookshop can't stock them all, though they may have a few titles. You will find a selection of titles in a specialized educational bookshop, but its best to go along to your local children's library, and look for the Easy Readers, or Junior Fiction section. They stock a lot of titles, and all have a high turn-round. If you have access to a school library, talk to the librarian – what is the school buying, which titles are most popular?

First of all, comes the idea. I'm often asked, 'Where do you get your ideas?' Presumably if you're reading this, you already have lots of ideas of your own. I'd say ideas come from anywhere. It's useful to have a notebook – jot down the odd idea as you're ironing, or washing up. It may not make a story but the seed is there. I do find – though it may not work for everyone – that a story can begin with an object, or observing something everyday.

For example *Mostly Magic* (Hamish Hamilton) began when I remembered an old bedspread which was brought out when we children had colds or measles or some other childish ailment. It was a bedspread with a Chinese pattern, which was oddly comforting. *The Digger* (Simon and Schuster) began when I noticed a hole in the road – and wouldn't it be odd if a kangaroo came up all the way from Australia?

Sometimes I'm asked to judge writers' groups competitions for children's writing. The stories that stand out are those which begin from a simple idea. I can recall one about the rubbish bags waiting to be collected in the street. Another began with just a long piece of string.

Don't throw out an idea. Maybe you've written a story which has been rejected. Save the idea – perhaps you can use one of the characters. Or take out an incident and build it up.

Spend time thinking about your characters. They must be real to you or they won't be real to the children. How do your characters react to say, their parents, school friends, brothers and sisters? You must like your characters (I've heard bestselling novelists say this, and it applies equally to the children's market).

Often, when I talk to schools, I'm asked which character of those in my books is my favourite. I usually say Allie (she appears in *The Wedding Day Scramble* and *Mostly Magic*, both published by Hamish Hamilton). She's well meaning and always in trouble. I explained to one group that I like her because she resembles my childhood self, who meant to do the right thing but didn't quite make it. A small boy in the front row sighed. 'That's just like me,' he said. It did sound as if it came from the heart.

Make sure your story is accurate. This sounds a fairly elementary thing to say, but children of around seven are very knowledgeable. They've watched a lot of TV, are very curious, and have a surprising amount of knowledge about the natural world. (Top marks to teachers who have encouraged and developed this interest in the environment.) So check every fact. This in itself is absorbing. For my latest book, *My Friend Robinson* (Hippo), which is for slightly older children, I had to find out about volcanoes, making musical instruments, and the life of Robinson Crusoe, just for starters.

My books about a plant-eating dinosaur (Hamish Hamilton) have to be thoroughly researched because dinosaurs are favourites with children, and most could do a *Mastermind* on the life and times of the iguanodon with no trouble at all.

My newest book about this character involved finding out about thunderstorms – so I went to the top and a phone call to the Met Office produced the information right away. But generally you'll find the information in your local library – the children's library non-fiction section will have any number of good information books, simply written.

It's a great help to try out your story on a group of children. I'm sometimes invited to talk at schools – I try out a story and go on to explain how the story becomes a finished book.

I find this very helpful indeed. So often something seems funny on the typewritten page, and the joke falls flat in the classroom. Or sometimes a joke you thought tame will produce gales of laughter. In *The Library Monster* (Hamish Hamilton), the baby dinosaur, a plant-eater, joins in Book Week at the local library, and creates havoc among the books (because paper comes from plants, of course). One line goes: 'The dinosaur had chosen a book on computers for its pudding.' Fairly mild humour, you'll agree. But whenever I reach this line in a storytelling session, it brings the house down. I've no idea why.

So you've written your first draft and possibly tried it out with children. The next thing is to write it again – and again. A lot of work for a 2,500-word reader? Well, maybe it is, but how much better and simpler the story will be the third or fourth time. When I visit schools, I usually take various versions of an MS – showing the cuts, the rewriting, the finished version.

This produces oohs and aahs from the children, and support from the teacher who has been trying to stress the importance of not being satisfied with first attempts.

Is it the right length? Is it simple enough? I usually do a reading test to check the age level. There are various tests you can do for language level. But you don't need to do this as long as you keep the sentences and paragraphs short. Look at the dialogue too. Is this how children speak? Is this how your characters – human or animal – would communicate? Read it out loud if you like.

Finally you send the MS to your chosen publisher. If you have done your research, you'll have a good knowledge of who publishes what. Aim at a particular series. (You can always send off for catalogues.)

It goes without saying that your MS should look clean and fresh – so many publishers receive tired-looking scripts that have been hawked round a dozen firms.

Put the length of the story on the front page. Tell the publisher you know the series and have written with it in mind. Then wait – sometimes two or three months. Publishers receive a lot of unsolicited MSS. But while you're waiting, start another story. Then when the publisher says, 'We liked this – have you any more?' you have something else to send.

Illustrations? I don't do my own – and neither should you, if you want to get your book accepted. Artwork tied to text (or vice versa) can be a handicap. Few publishers will take on both an untried author and an untried artist, unless the material is very very good. So don't encourage your friend or relative to provide the artwork for your book. The publisher will commission it.

A good artist will enhance the quality of your text. So if your book is accepted, you'll be offered a contract with a royalty which takes into account the artwork costs. It's only fair that the artist should receive a substantial fee or even share the royalty, because artwork is so important in this type of book.

So what are the rewards? They're not sensational, but steady. Books for the beginner reader sell mainly to libraries, so it's important to register for Public Lending Right – and the resulting payment can be a very pleasant surprise. PLR is an excellent barometer – because it tells you which books the children are borrowing themselves, which books they're actually choosing from the shelves, not being offered by teachers or parents.

The other rewards? Getting mail from young readers. It's great when they write to tell you they've enjoyed your book, and when they send drawings of your characters, or even their own stories. It's great when a reader takes the trouble to write from overseas – to think your book has been enjoyed in the remote Australian bush.

It's good too, when you're asked to talk to a library or school group and meet the readers face to face. Sometimes their letters of thanks are accompanied by candid comments. For example, 'I was very surprised when I saw you. I thought you'd be a lot younger.'

Generally, it's great writing for this age group – like everything worthwhile, it's hard work, but tremendously rewarding.

Anne Forsyth was born and educated in Scotland. Having worked in journalism and in educational publishing, she is now a freelance editor. She has published 15 children's books, mainly for the 5–8 age group – including the popular Monster *series (Hamish Hamilton), about a baby dinosaur, which has also been published in Japanese.*

What's in a Name?

Bill Bradley

Names are important to a fiction writer. A name conjures up an immediate image in the mind of the reader, but it must also fit the personality of the mental character the writer has created.

A fictional character called Tom Coffin will not create the same initial image in the mind of the reader as one named Duncan McKenzie. The writer, however, will be well acquainted with the character he has created. It is important that the two images, one in the writer's mind and one in the reader's, should be brought into line with each other as soon as possible. The choice of name is important because it is one of the first common reference points.

Distinctive names help to make characters easily distinguishable from each other. It is usually a mistake to have characters in the same story or novel with similar names such as Sally and Sandra, or Andrew and Anthony. In the early stages the reader might tend to confuse the two characters.

Even when carefully chosen, the same name can conjure up different images in the minds of different readers. A woman whose well-loved mother is called Rhoda may have quite a different conception of a character with that name than someone whose boyfriend was lured away by a Rhoda.

The origin of names can have an effect on the image they project. Biblical names such as Reuben and Aaron, or Rachael and Jessica will seem older and more staid to the reader than a Kevin or a Tracy.

Names carry geographical labels too. Shamus and Maura are Irish, Nerys and Morgan are Welsh, and Isla and Murdoch have an obviously Scottish flavour.

The period in which a story is set must also be taken into consideration. In the lists of recorded births in England and Wales right through from 1700 until 1925, John and William regularly competed for the first place in popularity. In 1988 John had dropped to 39th place and William to 47th. The most popular names given to male children in 1988 were Daniel and Christopher. In the same year in the USA the most popular name for boys was Michael (perhaps thanks to Michael Jackson).

Careless use of names can create anachronisms, as would happen if a character named Wendy was born before 1904, the year in which J M Barrie's *Peter Pan* first introduced the name.

The social class of a character can affect the choice of name, although this applies more to historical than contemporary work. For example, someone called Abigail would at one time have been immediately identified as a lady's maid.

Diminutives can be used to advantage in fiction. A character who normally addresses his wife or daughter as Pam could, in a moment of anger or displeasure, call her Pamela. One word can symbolize the mood of the character who is speaking.

Family names are just as important as first names. Most of our surnames have existed for at least 500 years and some of them still have geographical significance. A Morgan or a Meredith could have originated in Wales, a McGregor or a Cameron in Scotland – at least that is the initial impression the reader will get.

In the past many surnames gave a clear indication of where a person lived. In 1890 Henry Brougham Guppy published his *Homes of Family Names in Great Britain*. He made a particular study of the names of farmers, this being the group which tended to stay put more than others. He listed the Trickles as being natives of Cheshire, the Tricks and Trotts belonging to Devon and the Tinklers concentrated mainly in County Durham.

Surnames no longer have relevance to the occupations of their owners, although this is how many of them originated. Someone named Barker would have been employed in the leather trade dealing with wood bark, a Mercer would have dealt in silks and similar fabrics.

Place names can be a useful source of inspiration for fictional surnames – John Lancaster or Mary Sutton for example. A search through a gazetteer can produce more imaginative and colourful names if required.

Nicknames can be quite useful to novelists, and can provide clues to the personality or appearance of the character. The reader needs to be familiar with the nickname before it is used indiscriminately, otherwise one can be misled or confused into thinking a new character has appeared. An early explanation is often given, describing why the nickname was bestowed. In *The Old Curiosity*

Shop Dickens gives a rather long-winded description of the physical characteristics which led to a character named Harris sometimes being called 'Short', sometimes 'Trotters' and sometimes 'Short Trotters'. In *Little Men* (1871) Louisa M. Alcott tells the reader 'His name is George but we call him "Stuffy" 'cause he eats so much.'

Suitable names for places and locations require careful thought. If a real place is used the writer must ensure accuracy when describing it. The credibility of an otherwise excellent story would be destroyed for the knowledgeable reader by mention of 'the sandy beaches of Sorrento' or 'the spires of York Minster', neither of which exist.

Some authors create their own names for places, as Samuel Butler did when he turned 'nowhere' into 'Erewhon' for the name of his imaginary Utopian country.

J B Priestley created 'Bruddersford' out of Bradford and Huddersfield. Created names need to sound authentic and can often be produced by combining parts of two actual names, as for example, 'Colbourne' from Colchester and Eastbourne. Convincing names for towns, cities, villages, even countries, can be created in this way, thus avoiding the need for accurate geographical description – but care should be taken to check that such a place does not actually exist.

Names of businesses and house names are used in many fictional works, forming part of the image-making element of the fiction writer's craft. Such names can give the reader clues to the personality of the character who named the house or business. What sort of doctor would name his house 'Kilmeny'? What kind of man would live in a house named 'The Belfry' if his name was Batt? What sort of family would live at 'Honeywell Farm'? A glance through the yellow pages can reveal unusual names for businesses, such as the 'Klassy Klippers' hairdressing salon, the 'Kamikaze Driving Academy' or the 'Bees Knees' boutique.

Names for pets can be important, either because they are appropriate to a particular pet, or because they reveal a characteristic or attitude of the person who gave them their name. What sort of person would call his Pekinese 'Tiger' or his dachshund 'Lofty'? Rudyard Kipling features a dog called 'Blast' in his novel *On Greenhow Hill*, explaining that it was so named because it was the sole survivor from a litter which got caught in an explosion.

Boats, cars and other personal possessions can also be given names which reflect the personality or special interest of their owners. A boat named 'Girl Friend' or 'Lust' could indicate an owner with a special type of interest. One named 'Say When' or 'Bottoms Up' would indicate a different interest.

Public house and other names can be woven into a story to add to its colour and texture. A lonely moorland road is an obvious site for 'The Silent Inn'. 'The Fleece' is likely to be somewhere in the Yorkshire woollen district. 'The Alice Hawthorn', named after a famous racehorse, is likely to be near a racecourse. Careful use of appropriate names in any category adds authenticity.

Many authors use pen names. Some use more than one, perhaps because they write novels in different genres or categories, or because one of their pen names is under contract to a particular publisher.

There is no copyright in pen names, so anyone could offer a novel under the name of Jeffrey Archer or Catherine Cookson without infringement.

However, no publisher would be likely to accept work written under such a name, and if it did appear in print the person using the name could be faced with an injunction to prevent further use; and in some cases could be presented with a claim for compensation from the person already using it.

The Brontë sisters adopted the pen names of Currer, Acton and Ellis Bell because, at the time they were writing, it was thought that readers would be prejudiced against women writers. More recently the few men who have successfully written for Mills and Boon have hidden behind a female pen name.

Pen names are sometimes used if writers feel that their real names are unattractive, they wish to conceal their identity, or they merely don't like their given name. George Orwell's real name was Eric Blair. He is reported to have said that it took him 30 years to wear off the effect of being called Eric.

A pen name may conceal the fact that two or more writers have been responsible for the work. The earlier novels of the popular writer Jessica Stirling were written by two people.

The subject of names is one which has fascinated writers and academics for many years and dozens of books have been written on various aspects of the subject. One which is particularly interesting and informative is *The Guinness Book of Names* by

Leslie Dunkling. Besides having almost 200 pages of information about all sorts of names, the book has a three-page bibliography listing more than 150 other books which deal with particular aspects of the subject, including *Titled Trains in Great Britain* by Cecil J. Allen, *Naming the Hindu Child* by Dwarka Nath, *A Dictionary of Pub Names* by L. A. Dunkling and G. Wright, and *Pseudonyms* by J. F. Clarke.

One which may be of particular interest to a novelist struggling to find the right name for a newly born character is E. C. Smith's *Naming Your Baby*.

Using the right names in your novel is important. Emile Zola, in *Dr Pascal*, wrote: 'I always judge a young author by the names which he bestows on his characters. If the names seem to be weak or unsuitable to the people who bear them, I put the author down as a man of little talent, and am no further interested in the book.'

Bill Bradley writes successfully in a number of fields: some 400 of his short stories and articles and three of his novels have appeared in print. His only – so far – broadcast radio play has been repeated twice. As a tutor, he has helped many writers to achieve publication.

Tips for Writing Short Stories

Syd Bounds

A tale 'leaves in the mind . . . a sense of the fullest satisfaction'. These are the words of Edgar Allan Poe, whom some consider the father of the short story.

I don't believe many of us would disagree with this statement. Obviously, if we want to please readers, and editors, we need to satisfy them. So let's take a closer look at what this means, and ways of achieving our target.

To satisfy, as defined by my dictionary, is: 'To fulfil an obligation; to meet expectations; to gratify a desire'.

Some years ago, you may remember, there was a fashion for stories with only a beginning and a middle. (Perhaps their authors confused fiction with real life?) You don't see many like that today because readers weren't satisfied.

A short story must have an ending that meets the reader's expectations. It should not just fade away; loose ends must be tied and explanations given. Only then will editors come back for more.

One way to do this is to open with a problem, and close with its solution. The solution should be logical, but never obvious in the body of the story; neither should it rely on coincidence. Instead, your main character must solve the problem by his own effort; and the more ingenious he is the better.

Another method is to make sure that your story builds up to a single dominant emotion; when your reader experiences this emotion at the finishing line, he or she will be happy.

Or you can make use of a strong theme, such as 'Blood is thicker than water'. If you prove your theme by the end of the story, again readers will be content.

Warning: this theme should be implied by your storyline and revealed through character, not stuck on as an afterthought like the moral to a Victorian novel.

Another technique is to use a sympathetic character who wins through against all odds. To achieve this, you need to arrange the nature of the conflicts so that, in reacting to them, your hero reveals his main character trait. Do this consistently with each scene – a scene is one unit of conflict and reaction – and you will prove his trait and, once again, please the reader.

The story with a twist in its tail has always been popular. Unfortunately, this type of story has been overdone in recent years and editors are not easily surprised. Professional writers use a double twist. First comes the twist we don't mind readers guessing; then a final twist we hope they won't.

Years ago, an editor told me: 'I want your stories because they are properly rounded.'

What he meant, I think, is what I call the 'circular' tale: like a snake swallowing its own tail, beginning and end join up. This guarantees reader satisfaction, providing you've involved them emotionally along the way.

There are three steps involved in achieving this:

First: At the plotting stage, make sure you build up to a dramatic climax and stop. Anything after this is anti-climactic, unnecessary and boring.

Second: When writing the story and you approach the end, stop and re-read the opening before you write that final paragraph. Then, memory refreshed, write your ending to link up.

Third: If possible, use the same words or phrasing to punch it home. A useful tip is to repeat the full name of your protagonist in the last paragraph (assuming you used this to introduce him).

So next time you are analysing published stories, study beginning and finishing paragraphs.

Let's see how it works in practice with a few examples.

This is the opening of *Dark Spot*, a science-fiction story for boys:

The intercom light flashed. Cliff North, ace newscaster of the Universe, flipped the master key.

'Yes. What is it?'

Doc Summers' clipped tones answered: 'Dark Spot dead ahead, Cliff.'

The story ends with:

Cliff North grinned and slapped Doc Summers on the back.

'Full speed for Earth, Doc. I have a story for the Universe *– the secret of the Dark Spot!'*

My next example comes from *The Haunted Tower*, a ghost story for children. It opens with:

'That?' said Uncle Harry. 'That's one of the old telegraph towers.'

And ends with:

Sue said, 'Tom saved the tower, didn't he? He proved that he and the semaphore were important. He's at rest now.'

Note that this story begins and ends with dialogue, another variation on our theme.

My last example, *The Pauper's Feast*, comes from an adult terror anthology. This uses the 'biter-bit' pattern, where an unpleasant character comes to a sticky end; yet another method of satisfying readers.

The story opens:

With a plump hand resting on a mahlstick, he lettered his initials – JVL – with some care to the finished painting.

And closes:

On a smudged sketch she caught sight of the initials: JVL. As she scrambled to her feet to run from the court, her movement disturbed an army of retreating rats.

Do you see how the deliberate repetition of initials forms a link between beginning and end?

So remember your target and forget about pleasing yourself. Your job is not only to amuse, surprise and entertain the reader, but to 'leave in the mind . . . a sense of the fullest satisfaction'.

Syd Bounds has sold all kinds of short stories including confessions, juvenile, science fiction and horror. They have been published in Britain and reprinted in Australia, Italy, Poland, Sweden and the USA. Several have been adapted for radio or TV. Recent publications include stories in Mystery for Christmas *(O'Mara Books) and* Fantasy Booklet *magazine.*

2

WRITING NON-FICTION

Despite the undoubted attractions – and possible *kudos* – of fiction writing, many writers are better advised to start with non-fiction. If nothing else, the competition is usually less.

Look along the shelves of your local newsagent: almost every one of those magazines uses at least half a dozen articles to each short story – and a large number of magazines carry no fiction at all. Look at publishers' lists of new books: overall there are three or four non-fiction books for every novel – and a first non-fiction book has a far better chance of being accepted than does a first novel.

A fiction writer needs a creative imagination. A non-fiction writer – of articles and books alike – needs a steady flow of new ideas. A non-fiction writer has to keep coming up with something new. Alison Bremner suggests ten practical – and successful – ways of 'Finding Ideas' for future articles. Marian Hardless too offers half a dozen suggestions on getting fresh ideas among her practical 'Twenty Tips for Article Writers'.

Editors, always on the lookout for ways to improve the appearance of their magazines, will also welcome what Raymond Palmer calls 'Sidebars that Sell'. He explains how to add a *sidebar* – and increase your fee.

But many writers will want to progress from article writing to book writing. Because it is so packed with hard advice, I have included one of my own articles in this selection. 'Selling a Non-Fiction Book' is a very different process to selling a novel or an article. The good news is that you sell the book before you write it – *and* get some money 'up front'. (The bad news? It's hard work; and few of us get to sell any film or TV rights.)

And to balance the 'How To' advice in my piece, Derek Gregory 'tells all' about his extremely successful experience in 'Tackling the Textbook'. (Why, oh why, didn't I write a school textbook instead of a management text?)

Five down-to-earth, practical pieces on non-fiction writing – and all by successful writers.

Finding Ideas

Alison Bremner

It has been said that a journalist is not someone who knows everything but is merely someone who knows where to get the facts. And the ideas. And once you have an idea you have one, perhaps ten, articles.

But where do you get the ideas from? 'Be original', they tell you. 'Get a fresh angle'. But how? Listed below are ten ways of finding ideas that sell.

1. You don't have to be somewhere exotic to be filled with new ideas. As soon as you walk out of your house they are all around you. As Ogden Nash said, 'The place you're at is your habitat. Everywhere else you're a foreigner'.

Start to think like a foreigner. Question everything – Why? Where? What? When you are on holiday, make use of the new environment. You don't need to explore the ideas until you get home. I was recently on a train to Penzance. Snaking along the Torbay seafront my friend pointed out the lines of Victorian beach huts. 'See those,' she said, 'they're worth a fortune. They've become fashionable. And expensive. It's ridiculous'. I opened my notebook and scribbled, 'Beach huts –? Future property investment!'

2. Use your local police station. Explain that you are a writer and would be interested in any stories they can give you. Arrange to visit or telephone on a regular basis.

One story I got was about a local resident who had reported his pet tortoise stolen from his garden. Besides making a good story for the local paper it triggered off an idea for a feature on pet insurance and another on unusual pets.

If the story has wider interest you could try ringing one of the national papers. Ask for the news desk but have your piece ready (a couple of paragraphs in news style) because if they like it they'll put you straight through to the copy-takers. Often you get paid a small sum (about £25) even if they don't want your idea. After all, they want you to ring them in future – they need news.

3. Scan local newspapers. Not just yours. Ask friends who live in other areas to save theirs too. File interesting cuttings. Under 'Birthdays' I found 'Local artist – 88 years old today'. I realised that she was born in 1900, so I wrote to her. She was delighted to talk about her paintings and her life. The profile was accepted by the same newspaper.

4. Arrange to meet other writers as regularly as possible. Apart from workshops and writers' circles it is useful to have someone with whom you can discuss your latest projects, exchange new markets and names of editors; share magazines, newspapers and contacts and talk through your ideas. Just discussing them rather than thinking about them can lead to the angle you need.

5. Advertisements: even the classifieds can trigger off an idea for a feature. 'Wedding dress size 12 perfect condition £20'. That made me wonder how many people buy second-hand wedding dresses. How much are brides prepared to pay for a dress? What do the top designers charge? List, research and cost everything you'd need for a wedding and you've got a good springtime article.

6. Mailing lists. The average house-holder hates being on them. Writers should make the most of them. Get on the lists of the P.R. agents that interest you. Most companies, organisations and high street stores have a P.R. agent (if not they have a press department).

Telephone or write asking to be put on their mailing list. Explain that you are a writer (you don't need to have been published). They will be delighted to help because you may be able to give them publicity. This is what they want.

They are also an excellent source of photographs and transparencies, quotes and interviews, in some cases, even trial products.

7. Statistics. Jot down facts and figures you hear on the news or documentaries. They make articles more interesting and topical and they give you ideas.

The Population Census and Surveys Office (Tel: 071–242 0262) deal with population related statistics and will send you figures (e.g. marriage/divorce) as they are released.

8. Listen to conversation around you. Two elderly ladies sitting behind me on the bus: 'Terrible isn't it, I can remember when bread cost nine pence – and that was in the old money'.

I gazed out of the window and thought about it. How long ago would a loaf have cost 9d? How much did milk and butter cost? How much did a house or car or newspaper cost? Was it in my lifetime? I got off the bus and went to the library. The point is if you (or those around you) are asking questions, there are plenty more who would be interested in the answers.

9. Scan notice boards and leaflets. Reference libraries are a good source. Recently I picked up a pamphlet suggesting I earn some extra money by taking in a lodger. By the end of the day I had sold the idea ('Are you really better off?') to the Choices – Money section of the *Guardian* and was researching a commissioned article.

Months before I had found a similar leaflet advising people in financial difficulties of where to get help free of charge. I was surprised that the services mentioned were available to anyone. I researched further and sent an 'on spec' article to the *Guardian*. This was the first one of mine they published.

10. Thumb through an edition of the Pears Cyclopaedia (in your local reference library). The Chronicle of Events section starts with prehistory and progressively gets more comprehensive as it approaches the twentieth century. Apart from being ideal for anniversary articles it does mean you can plan them (and sell them) before they even become topical. And with monthly magazines you do need to work that far ahead.

Alison Bremner is a registered nurse, freelance writer and training consultant now living in Sydney, Australia. While living in England, Alison's work was frequently seen in The Times, *the* Guardian, Practical Health *and* Slimming *and* Writers' Monthly. *She was also the travel writer for* Metropolitan Magazine *in London between 1986 and 1988.*

Twenty Tips for Article Writers

Marian Hardless

Article writing is a bit like juggling with 12 balls. A few ideas are just surfacing, while some are being researched or written out in rough as others are finalised and submitted. Or re-written and re-submitted. The successful article writer needs to keep an eye on all these things, making sure that there is not so much record-keeping, research and administration going on that nothing is actually finished. Here are 20 tips to help you succeed with your articles.

Ideas
1. Keep an 'I could have written that' file, containing recent examples of magazine articles you should have thought of first. Can you get another angle on the idea for the same magazine or use it as a starting point for an article aimed at a different market?
2. Never waste an opportunity to browse through magazines in shops, libraries, waiting rooms and at friends' houses and write down any good ideas which strike you. The magazines you buy should be thoroughly toothcombed for inspiration. One or two ideas which you act on are better than dozens which you shelve.
3. Study the Market News columns in *Writers' Monthly* and use its suggestions. Buy or send off for specimen copies of any publications which might be in your line. Then get in early with a preliminary letter, article or list of outlines, whichever seems most appropriate. The editor of a new magazine needs to build up a bank of articles, so find out how you can help him or her.
4. Keep an ideas notebook for random jottings. People's comments, radio and TV programmes, newspapers, magazines and books and your own musings can all provide article ideas. Write them all down, but go through the list regularly, pruning it and using the best ideas.
5. Write a list of follow-up ideas on the carbon copy of each of your articles. You almost always need to edit out some of your research material as you write up the final version – what's left

will provide starting points for other pieces, so record the ideas while they're fresh in your mind.

6. Try, where possible, to develop an article into a series. If the idea is sound you may well sell the series as easily as the one-off article and get a chance to write regularly for that market.

Working methods

7. An organized work schedule helps to make the best use of time. When writing up one article have several more at the planning and research stage, because a lot of time can elapse waiting for replies to queries or trying to contact a particular expert. Leave some time each week for responding to new ideas, doing market study and dealing with post and administration.

8. Never shirk the rules for submitting a presentable manuscript – double-spaced typing on A4 paper, wide margins, a word count, and no pages with more than a couple of corrections. I only realised how many would-be writers still don't do these things when an editor congratulated me recently on my 'nice clean copy'. It makes all the difference!

9. Keep your research on specialist topics up to date and go through your files regularly, throwing out old material. Ploughing through yellowing bundles of ancient cuttings in search of current facts is not an efficient use of time.

10. Get an answerphone if you ever leave the house during working hours. The first one or two extra commissions it earns you will pay for it and your editors will come to trust you as an author who can always be contacted. They may need a photo or more information before scheduling your article. If the phone goes unanswered they'll be tempted to fill the space with someone else's work.

11. Order a box of sticky labels printed with your name, address and phone number. They make your articles look professional and transform ordinary writing paper into headed notepaper. If you have a second batch printed without the phone number you can also use them for SAEs.

Record keeping

12. An efficient records system is vital for article writers because of the number of manuscripts produced. One method is a card index, divided into sections. Use a card for each article to keep

track of the magazine(s) it has been sent to and the outcome. Keep one section for payments and expenses, another for up-to-date addresses and contacts and another for ideas.

13. Make notes on your dealings with each magazine. Jot down the findings of your market study and note ideas for possible future submissions. If you also record each article submitted together with any helpful comments made by the editor on accepting or returning it you will gradually build up an accurate picture of what is required by that particular market.

14. Keep a cuttings file, mounting each article opposite the front page of the magazine it came from. Make photocopies of your work to enclose when trying a new market and take the file with you if you are invited to meet an editor in person.

Time savers

15. Make good use of preliminary letters, outlining the proposed length and content of your article. Even if an editor doesn't commission the piece, an indication that he or she is interested in seeing it means it's a far better bet than an article sent in cold. And you might get helpful advice about the required angle or format which ups your chance of acceptance considerably.

16. Never waste a rejected article. Re-write it and re-submit it elsewhere in the hope of getting an acceptance cheque in return for your time and effort.

17. Research the usual format for your type of article in the magazine you're aiming at. Does the editor like checklists or tables of facts in separate boxes? How long are the paragraphs? Do most articles occupy a double spread or are shorter pieces preferred? Work out the rules and follow them to the letter!

18. Try using follow-up lists. When you receive an acceptance write a polite note expressing your pleasure and asking whether the editor would like to see more of your work. Enclose a list of three or four suggestions with an indication of length and a brief outline of the content. And don't forget the SAE!

Dealing with editors

19. Do everything you can to smooth an editor's job and *always* do what you have said you will. No matter that they keep your copy for six months, then telephone at 3.30 needing a photo in the post that night. Provide it, whatever the inconvenience. And if there is a truly unavoidable delay phone or write an immediate apology and state when the material will be arriving. Then stick to your word.

20. Do not phone a busy editor unnecessarily. But if he or she should ring you, use the opportunity to your advantage. After answering the query, sound out one or two new ideas and try to pick up hints about what is required in the near future. But remain businesslike, brief and to the point.

Marian Hardless writes three regular columns: a weekly children's page for the Mid-Somerset series of newspapers, a humorous diary for Mother and Baby *and a 'Writers' Corner' page for* Amstrad PCW. *She contributes to a variety of other publications, specialising in education and in humour. She also tutors writing classes for beginners.*

Sidebars that Sell

Raymond Palmer

Editors love sidebars. Sidebars are a plus factor when an editor considers whether to buy an article. If he has a choice between two very similar articles, the one with a sidebar or two is more likely to get the nod. He may also pay more for it!

So what is a sidebar?

A sidebar is a short, self-contained item that relates to the main article. Editors often take a short piece or two out of an article to make sidebars. But they appreciate writers who provide their own.

When I wrote an article on 'Discovering Hemingway's Spain' I included a sidebar listing hotels where he stayed, bars where he drank and some of his favourite restaurants. So far, editors in Britain, the USA, South Africa and Malaysia have liked the piece and the sidebar enough to buy them.

I always try to find a sidebar or two to accompany my articles. Think of the sidebar as a side dish to the main course, something that adds a little spice or freshness.

But don't go overboard. Most articles can benefit from one or two sidebars; only very long and serious articles need more.

The only rules to sidebars are that they must be short, tightly written, and relate to the main article. The three main types are the list, the quiz and the prose piece.

Lists take many forms – numbered or unnumbered. With numbered lists, the favourite number seems to be 10. Just think of the top 10 records, 10 best films, and the 10 best (or worst) dressed men or women. After 10, the most favoured numbers seem to be 5, 6, or 12. Other numbers just don't seem right.

But an article on luck, for example, could use 'Seven Lucky Charms' and '13 Unlucky Superstitions'. Use your imagination and see if a different number or two relates to the main story.

Lists are easy to create since you can list almost anything: do's and don'ts, the best this or that, myths, hints, tips, warnings.

Items can be set off by numbers, bullets, ticks, asterisks, or other typographical devices.

Quiz sidebars are popular with both editors and readers and can be serious or humorous. There are various kinds according to the way they are answered: true or false; A, B, or C; yes or no; always, sometimes, never; or some other form. Remember to provide answers and a method of scoring and tell what the scores mean. With a serious quiz, make sure the ratings are accurate.

If your article is about a subject widely misunderstood, a quiz can show readers how little they know about it and give them a reason to read the article.

Prose sidebars are just that – a block of text broken out of the main article. Placed in a box or panel, it gets extra attention and can focus on one aspect of your subject.

The most common is the service sidebar, detailing where to get more information. Most articles in *The Sunday Times* 'Travel' section are accompanied by a services sidebar telling how readers can get to the destination or duplicate a trip.

Sidebars may also include information, for example on currency exchange, inoculation and visa requirements. Other sidebars give useful information about the destination: the local cuisine, shopping guides, side trips, or useful phrases in the local language.

Service sidebars can be used with many articles – not only travel ones.

An article on home security can use sidebars on how to contact the local crime prevention officer, or list firms and organisations providing advice.

Another popular form of sidebar is the news flash, outlining latest developments and what the future may bring. While normally this material would be carried in the main article, it gives the piece a feeling of immediacy – of being on top of the news – if you break it out into a sidebar.

A sidebar for an article on traffic problems could detail current research and the sort of solutions it might produce. An article on a disease could use a sidebar detailing treatments being developed to offer sufferers new hope.

While the news flash sidebar looks to the future, background sidebars look to the past. This form is useful with major topics which have developed over a long period. Instead of slowing the

Ten reasons why you should use sidebars
1. Sidebars help you to organise long articles. If there's something that needs to go in but spoils the flow, turn it into a sidebar.
2. Sidebars can save material you don't want to lose when you have to cut your article. If the section you have to cut can stand on its own, turn it into a sidebar.
3. Editors like sidebars because readers enjoy them and they help improve the look of a magazine.
4. Sidebars are short and easy to read and often tempt readers into reading the main article.
5. Art editors and layout men like them because sidebars enable them to solve layout problems and to use borders, panels, tinted backgrounds and colour creatively.
6. Sidebars liven up the page, bringing variety to a mass of text, and making your article more attractive and compelling.
7. Sidebars enable you to focus in on the heart of your article in a way readers can relate to.
8. Sidebars make you appear more professional as a writer.
9. Sidebars help sell your articles.
10. Sidebars can bring bigger cheques.

The sidebar which accompanied this article

flow of your article with necessary background detail, boil it down into a sidebar.

The spotlight sidebar, on the other hand, looks to the present. This focuses on one current aspect of your article and puts the spotlight on it. This form is like a mini-article, completely self-contained, and is usually the longest form of sidebar.

It may focus on the one person doing most about the problem dealt with in your article, or one person who suffers from the problem. Whatever you focus on, it should be a microcosm example, a small corner that illuminates the whole.

The specification sidebar is another form editors and readers find useful. This gives specific details about goods or services mentioned in the article. An article on holiday insurance, for example, could have a sidebar comparing premiums charged and coverage offered by various insurance companies.

A final form of sidebar is the 'how to': how to do something connected with the main article. How to eat with chopsticks, how to paper a ceiling, how to re-pot plants, how to make your own this, that or the other. These can often be illustrated by the art editor with photos or line drawings.

There are doubtless other forms of sidebar that you will come across while leafing through newspapers and magazines, or that you may think of for yourself.

Keep sidebars in mind when researching and writing. Not only will they help to solve some of your organising and writing problems but they will endear you to editors and help you sell more articles.

Raymond Palmer became a full-time freelance in 1967 after 20 years as a staff journalist – mainly as writer and editor with Reuters and Associated Press. His articles have been published in magazines and newspapers in Britain and all over the world, particularly in America. His book, The Making of a Spy, *was published in Britain and America.*

Selling a Non-Fiction Book

Gordon Wells

We all keep reading that it's easier to get a non-fiction book published than a fiction one. How do you go about it? Let me explain.

First, you need a subject – about which you know a lot. This is clearly important. After all, who would want to read a book by you, if you don't know what you are talking about?

As soon as his/her name appears on the book cover, a non-fiction author takes on the mantle of 'Expert'. And experts can't be wrong.

In very general terms, non-fiction books can be biographies (plus a few autobiographies); travel books (which should either be 'You can experience the same delights' or something akin to a biography); history books (again, often somewhat similar to a biography); and 'How To' books. 'How To' books cover a multitude of subjects – from management to marquetry, from writing to rolling-pin collecting, from bell-ringing to fell-walking.

Unless you are an historian and/or are prepared to spend years delving into the archives, you are unlikely to write a saleable biography. Unless you swim the Atlantic single-handed on your back, you are unlikely to sell your autobiography. (It's not impossible, but the odds against success are great.) And everyone wants to write the conventional 'Guide to' type of travel book. Many are called, but few unknowns are chosen.

However most of us have a hobby, a skill, or a trade. And over the years, we will have learnt a whole lot about it. If we are good at it, we can probably sell a non-fiction book about it.

Let's concentrate on the broad territory of the 'How To' book. And for the sake of an example, let's say we are going to write about Widget Collecting.

First, we must think about the possible market for such a book. Is widget collecting a popular activity or are widgets as rare as green dogs and widget collectors even rarer? If so, you and your colleague are the only likely buyers of your proposed book. The two of you are not a big enough market to make the book publishable. So you would need to think again.

But let's be more optimistic. Widget collecting is the new *thing*. There are lots of widgets to be picked up at street markets and there is a lot of interest in them. And you have one of the best collections of widgets in the whole of England.

Not only have you a fine collection but, because of your longstanding interest in widgets, you have researched the history of widget-making both in this country and abroad. This is beginning to sound like a worthwhile subject for a book.

From where did you gather all your knowledge about widgets? From books? Are these books still in print? Are there lots of books already about widget collecting? If so, no one will be interested in a new book.

Again, we are lucky. There have only been a couple of new books on widget collecting since 1963; all other books on the subject are far older. You searched the secondhand bookshops to find them.

You need to do more checking though. Call at your local library and look up widgets in the non-fiction subject index. Make sure that you know all the books it lists. Ask the librarian whether there are many more books on the subject – or if there are any new widget books in the pipeline.

Now, think about these two recent books on widget collecting. How can you make your book different? Study the two books and think about this. Maybe one of the books is very academic and theoretical; you could easily make yours practical and down to earth.

The other current book may be very good. But you don't like the way it is written or set out; it may look more boring than it really is. Make your book better looking and easier to understand. Or restrict your book to the collecting of cheaper widgets and attract a wider readership.

The final piece of research is to find out if there are any magazines dealing with widget collecting. If it doesn't have its own specialist magazine, is the subject dealt with regularly in other collectors' magazines? Does widget collecting feature in the small ads? Are there shops specializing in antique widgets?

The answers to these questions will begin to give you an idea of the interest in widget collecting. You need this information to convince a publisher that there is a market for your book.

Now think about the book itself. Think about what you are going to put in it.

Take a blank sheet of paper and head it WIDGETS. (You must spend some time trying to think up a catchy, yet descriptive title. Keep it short.)

The next part is hard grind. What are you going to write about? Try listing what you know about widgets:

- Prices. Which ones are bargains and which are over-priced.
- How and where they are made.
- How best to store and display a collection.
- The history of widget development.
- Foreign widgets (can you find out more about them?).
- How best to start a collection. Where are the best places to pick up good cheap widgets.
- What widgets are used for, and how.

Dig a bit deeper into your memory. You may need more than that for a book. Ah yes . . .

- You know the history of the inventor of the widget, John Smith.

Look over the list. These different aspects of the widget would surely make a reasonable set of chapter headings. And that is what you are initially working towards.

You have listed all the aspects of widget collecting that you can think of, but have you covered **all** possible aspects? You may need to broaden your own knowledge, by research, in order to cover the subject fully.

Go back to the two recent books on widget collecting. Compare their chapter headings with your ideas. Do they cover a broader field than you? Shouldn't you too include the aspects they have but you don't? You may decide **not** to follow them in their coverage – but you must be able to justify that decision.

If you are satisfied that your coverage of the subject is complete, sort your chapter ideas into a logical sequence. At the same time, think up short – three or four word – chapter titles.

Here are my chapter titles in sequence:

1. Why collect widgets?
2. What are widgets?
3. The widget story.
4. John Smith – widget-maker.
5. How widgets are made.
6. Foreign widgets.
7. Starting your widget collection.
8. Displaying your widget collection.
9. Expanding your widget collection.

That looks reasonable. You need to be able to write about 4,000 words (or more) under each of those chapter headings to make a worthwhile book. 35,000 words is around the minimum length for a non-fiction book.

Now, you have to write the synopsis. This outlines what you will write under each of the chapter headings.

You should aim at writing, in almost note form, 60–70 words about each chapter content. For example:

4. John Smith – widget-maker
Born 1803, Wakefield of craftsman family. After school, trained and worked as corn dolly maker. In spare time, whittled. Seen at this, by champion Yorkshire whittler Albert Ramblebottom, who trained him well. Later, was given a Yugoslavian widget and copied it. Demand grew. So did skill. J Smith improved widget design beyond recognition and even found a new use for them. 1883 appointed Widget-maker Royal. J Smith widgets very rare – collectors' items.

Write like this on each of the chapters in the book. While writing the synopsis, think whether you will be able to expand the synopsis to the necessary minimum of 4,000 words. (Think of it in roughly 500 word sections. Can you write 500 words about John Smith's early life, before he left school? And will it be of interest?)

You may need to revise your thinking as you write the synopsis. Maybe one topic will make two chapters and another be better tagged on the end of another chapter. Retain a flexible approach. Satisfy yourself that you can produce 9 or 10 chapters, each about 4–5,000 words long, that will interest budding widget collectors.

The synopsis done, you must prepare a brief description of the book's objective, a plug for yourself as the ideal writer for the book, and an assessment of the market – the need and the competition – for the book.

All your initial research now comes into its own. Don't hide your light under any bushels – be pushy. Sell yourself and your idea for the book.

You are the best writer in the country to write a book such as you are proposing. You have already written articles about it (enclose one perhaps) and you have already had a book published on your collection of dustbin lids. You know more about widgets – at the relevant, collector level – than anyone else. (And you possess the biggest and best collection.) Your book will be better than its competitors – for the reasons we discussed earlier. You know that there is a big untapped demand for such a book.

Put all that in a 500 word single-sheet assessment. Work hard on that single sheet. A lot will depend on it. You have got to grab the publisher's attention with that page; the synopsis is almost of secondary importance.

Now, at last, you are ready to go. Decide on an appropriate publisher. That sounds easy? It isn't. My latest book, *The Book Writer's Handbook* (Allison & Busby) may give you some ideas on which publishers to approach. *The Writers' & Artists' Yearbook* (A&C Black) and *The Writers' Handbook* (MacMillan/Pen), also list publishers.

Who published your book on dustbin lids? Try them first of course. Who publishes other books on different sorts of collections? Who deals in craft books? (Widget making is a home craft. Crafts-people may well also collect.) Who published the other books in your collection – and on the library shelves? They may take another book if it really is from a different viewpoint.

Write – very briefly – to the first on your list of likely publishers. Say that you are proposing to write a book about widgets, and that you enclose a brief synopsis and assessment of the objectives and market for the book. Ask if they would be interested in such a book. Enclose a sae – and wait.

While you are waiting, draft a couple of chapters – it doesn't matter which ones, but not chapter 1 which introduces the subject. Don't go beyond draft stage. Don't write more than one or two chapters until you get a firm contract from a publisher. But most publishers will want to see a couple of sample chapters before they give you a contract.

I wouldn't send the samples with the initial assessment and synopsis. Apart from the postage costs, the publisher may wish to discuss the content and coverage before he sees the samples – which could lead to redrafting them.

Will an agent be of help in selling a non-fiction book like this? In my view, no. Agents are most interested in non-fiction books by or about 'names'. It would be hard to interest an agent in this sort of book. No one makes a lot of money from the sort of 'How To' books you or I can write.

Follow these guidelines, approach the publishers direct and good luck.

Tackling the Textbook

Derek Gregory

How would you like to make money from writing and become moderately famous and respected?

How would you like to do this without the worry of character development, with a ready-made foolproof plot, and not even have to provide a happy ending?

Finally, how would you like to have an army of unpaid helpers throughout the country (perhaps internationally) urging readers to buy your books?

You would? Well, so did I. And I achieved it by writing my first textbook in co-operation with a professional statistician. It became a bestseller. It has sold steadily for nearly 20 years; over 70,000 copies to date; netting me well over £20,000 at current prices.

And that is only *half* of what I should have received had I written it myself. Of course, to the latter sum you should add the stream of Public Lending Right earnings and, most recently, a substantial cheque for photocopying fees from the Authors' Licensing and Collecting Society.

Non-fiction book publishing is a huge field. Out of £2,711 million spent on books in 1987, only £257 million went on fiction sales.

I started on the road to success when as a novice teacher I was bemoaning the fact that no really decent, understandable, elementary book on statistics existed for my low level class.

Statistics wasn't my subject anyway. I am pretty ignorant of maths and I had been forced to take the class because they couldn't afford another part-time teacher. What I needed was an easy text for *myself* – never mind the students!

There wasn't one. I plodded through to June, keeping two weeks ahead of them for the whole nine months. I said a thankful goodbye to the class, but a big 'hello' to a course-sized pile of notes on elementary statistics.

I had culled these from a variety of intermediate textbooks and translated them into language that even a mathematical moron like myself could understand. They say the best way to learn a subject is to teach it. 'They' are right!

The rest is the brief monetary history I related above. It included, of course, writing to several well-known publishers in the field about my idea. I was amazed to find that most of them were extremely keen to encourage me. No rubbish about rejection slips so far.

Publishers of educational textbooks are easy to find. In fact the major publishing houses such as Heinemann and Macmillan advertise distinct divisions for this sector of their interests.

About half an hour's research in a good bookshop is all that is needed. Neither is there any nonsense about publishing styles. They will gladly send you a sheet laying out their house style requirements.

The research and marketing you need to do is quite simply to examine the products of competitors: those of similar level and subject to your intended book.

Notes should be made of chapters and contents, and topics covered. From this you can get a good idea of what to put in and leave out. After this you will need to write for syllabuses and some past question papers of the various institutes, if any, you intend your book to cover.

So far your research has revealed what experienced writers have successfully judged to be necessary in the particular field. No bad start.

The next stage is to update your textbook. Any textbook is outdated as soon as it is published. As a first-time author in the subject, you have this in-built advantage. It consists of modern factual revisions to examples and the re-ordering of contents, in the light of any syllabus changes. If, as I am suggesting, you tackle a textbook at the elementary level, this will hardly involve any earth-shattering changes.

But how can you make your textbook different? Why should you add to the existing market? The most decisive questions for potential publishers are twofold. First, how can they carve out part of the market enjoyed by their competitors? And second, how can they create an extension of the existing market?

These questions are answered by the author by: a) bringing your book up to date, b) writing it so that it can be better understood, c) writing it differently, titling and slanting your book to bring in extensions to the market.

Point a) has already been mentioned. With regard to b) in these days communication occupies a higher place than it has ever done in education and in world affairs.

Education for all means that any book which is easier to understand than its predecessor will be welcomed with open arms. At this level you are not trying to push outward the frontiers of knowledge.

As a writer, communication is your forte, or should be. And a sexy cover won't help. You are writing for what the economists call an 'informed market'. It is the **teachers**, not the pupils, who will recommend your book. Teachers are not principally in the entertainment business. Their main aim is simply to get a message across.

Which leaves c), writing it differently. My own effort was a book on statistics. Why not write it to appeal to the busy corporate executive (who usually leaves that sort of thing to the boffin boys who are regarded in the firm with reverence)?

We tried to do this by renaming our book *Statistics for Business* – making it evident that it wasn't confined to students.

Could it be written as *Statistics for Busy Housewives*? Well, perhaps not. But the more brutal *Statistics for Morons* might have a reasonable life. *Statistics on the Computer*, *Statistics for the Average Man*, *All You Need Know About Statistics*, *Statistics for the Hopeless Gambler* – you see, I am playing about with the ideas. It is called 'brainstorming'.

Approaching a publisher requires a brief statement about the angle of your book, a couple of specimen chapters, and a synopsis.

In my own case, the prime selling point was the absence of mathematical hieroglyphics. But wide professional institute coverage was also written in. There is a little extra work here. Publishers like to be reassured that they are not backing a hopeless cause (can you blame them?).

It is a good idea, and they often leave it to the author, to supply some figures. These are easily gathered by writing to the various professional institutes to find out how many of their students took the subject last year. Also by examining past examination results: How many attempted? How many failed?

I hope I'm not making this sound too easy. In my own case I

had done a good bit of spadework during the course, but the actual writing over the next nine months (still teaching full time) was quite interesting.

My co-author was only too anxious to explain 'knotty' points in painless English. Instead of 'living with' fictional characters, I saw the worried looks and dropped jaws of my students float before me every time I penned another point of explanation.

Here are some more basic pointers. First, it is a great bonus writing in English. You would be surprised at the foreign demand for textbooks in English, not only in countries like Australia and New Zealand, but in undeveloped countries like East Africa. My book has sold well in all of these places.

Secondly – you haven't got a PhD in the subject? So much the better! My theory is, the less you know about a subject at this level, the better your chance of communicating it to others, similarly ignorant. And I proved it in my own case. (Think of all those expertly written, incomprehensible, computer manuals!)

By overcoming your own problems of understanding you are better placed to solve the problems of others. It is the experts who should be kept out of this field. It all came so easily to them that many have not the patience to inspire basic understanding in ordinary mortals. This is where your creative writing gifts come in.

Another essential point to note: you will find your mass market in lower level work. Most of us have some GCE 'O' levels. Most of us have struggled with our own children. Many of us have done some teaching.

GCSE is the highest level you will write for. And remember, you teach to the middle ability of a class, not to the brightest and busiest little bees. Anything higher you can leave to those who live in the clouds. Anything higher and you will lose the mass market. The knowledge required would take years to achieve anyway.

You could earn more money by selling a short story to *Woman's Weekly* than an expert would normally make by turning his PhD thesis into an authoritative tome. He does it to put on his next job application form, not for immediate rewards.

The actual writing is best looked on as a series of 'boxes' to be filled. E.g. 'Title Pages', 'Table of Contents', 'Acknowledgements', 'Abbreviations', Chapters '1', '2', '3' . . . , 'Glossary', 'Index'.

Chapter contents are compiled from the syllabuses and arranged progressively. Within each chapter you could divide it into Explanation, Examples, Questions . . . but – you should be on your own by now.

The point I want to make is that by breaking it down into little sections you can easily tackle what might seem a monumental task, in weekly writing splurges.

Does this seem 'mechanical'? It is certainly not as soul-searching as creating fiction. The 'creativity' comes in when you communicate your thoughts, through prose, to the wondering child in your imagination.

If you are well versed in writing for children you can go lower than 'O' level. The sky's, or rather, the ground's the limit. Most teachers are too hard pressed to write textbooks. Most have not the writing skills anyway. They may dread putting pen to paper as much as you may dread standing in front of a class. If you really feel you have not even the basic knowledge you can team up with a teacher, as I did, and suggest joint authorship. Husband and wife team? Publishers like that sort of thing.

The production process is more complicated than that of the average novel. Space restrictions are things dictated by printers and by costs. These, of course, are related to possible markets and competitive prices.

It may be one thing to cut down or add a bit on to your romantic novel. It is less easy to vary the acreage of your average statistics book.

Unfortunately costs are paramount and, in the eyes of educational publishers, profits from lower level works are often regarded as subsidies for more prestigious (loss-making, but image-producing) academic ones.

It is said, for example, that the publishing house of Macmillan was bolstered for years from the profits of its *School Algebra*.

Illustrations are not usually a problem. The author will be asked to provide rough drawings and the publisher will usually accept responsibility for engaging a professional for the finished artwork.

Photographs, however, may well be asked for. Indexing, also, is a task bestowed on the author. Professional indexing is expensive and will cut into your royalties, so this is a chore you can easily undertake yourself.

Proof-reading should be meticulous. Mistakes will be deducted from your royalties! In my case it meant an eye-screwing scrutiny of mathematical symbols and tables. Figures are more tedious to proofread than words.

Much consultation may have to take place up to the galley-proof stage. Imagine my surprise when, after the full text of my statistics book had been accepted, I was politely asked by letter to cut it down by a third!

Of course I was appalled. I could hardly ask the examining bodies to cut down their syllabuses by a third! I toyed with the idea of cutting out every third word. Eventually I found a way, even if it did involve sacrificing most of those beautifully worked model questions at the back.

But one of the nicest things about writing a textbook is its long life. You *could* write a classic novel of course, and it *could* sell for years.

But a decent textbook has a much longer life than your average novel which sells barely more than 1,000 copies and the rot usually sets in after year one.

My textbook has been going for 20 years and is in its fourth edition. Which reminds me. It's ready for updating again!

Derek Gregory is an ex-polytechnic lecturer, now in his early sixties, who has begun a writing career which should have started 40 years earlier. He has published many articles and won several short story competitions. He is the editor of the Tees Valley Writer *magazine. One day he hopes to write a decent novel.*

3

WRITING DRAMA – AND POETRY

The other main areas of writing interest are, of course, writing drama and writing poetry. Can there be any writer who has not sat through what was, in their view, a poor TV or radio play – and vowed that they 'could write better with their eyes closed'? And the interest in writing poetry seems ever-alive and growing.

Without doubt, the big money-making areas for would-be dramatists are radio and TV. But it may be easier to break into drama by writing for the amateur stage. Freelance writer Mary Rensten interviewed David Campton, a leading writer for the amateur stage, who offers much helpful advice on 'Writing for Amateur Theatre'.

One field of amateur drama often overlooked by budding playwrights is the annual pantomime. Jackie Short offers practical advice on 'Writing a Pantomime' while Ann Stevens reports, in 'Oh No She Didn't!', on the problems she experienced in writing – and staging – her first panto. She says she'll do it again, so the tribulations clearly were not too disastrous.

Bill Bradley writes successfully in a number of different fields. Here, he offers advice on 'Creating Landscapes in the Mind' – how a radio writer has to spark the listeners' own imagination to picture the unseen scene. Following this, professional radio and TV comedy writer Jim Eldridge discusses different aspects of writing humour – and offers practical 'How To' advice – in 'The Joke's on You'.

Moving on to poetry, we have a real success story. It takes hard work – and a good idea – to get a non-fiction book accepted; it needs a lot of luck – and much talent – to get a first novel accepted. These problems are as nothing, though, compared with the chances of getting a book of poems published. Many poets end up publishing their own poems; the handful of commercial publishers of poetry are permanently inundated with offers of books of verse. It says a lot therefore, about Glyn Maxwell's poetry – and his persistence – that he is able to write, from personal experience, about 'Getting a Book of Poems Published'. It's well worth reading.

Writing for Amateur Theatre

Mary Rensten interviews David Campton

David Campton has written over 100 plays, for markets as diverse as radio, the professional theatre, television, schools, church dramatic societies and Women's Institutes.

'The elements they all have in common,' he says, 'are a sense of humour, a definite point of view (not to be confused with a "message"), compact construction, a touch of fantasy and a feeling for theatre.'

His work has been compared with that of Ionesco and Pinter and there is, on average, a production of at least one of his plays somewhere in the world every day.

His first published play, *Going Home*, was produced in Leicester in 1950 when he was working for the East Midlands Gas Board. He has since been a working playwright for nearly 40 years. With each new play Campton says, 'I take a deep breath . . . and go back to square one.

'In fact, I go back further than square one because there's this terrible jeering critic at the back of my mind that says, "You've used this idea before," which you tend not to have when you're starting out.'

The critic was certainly there when David began to write *Can You Hear The Music?*, a play about 'six mice listening to the Pied Piper and getting knocked off one by one'.

'You see, I'd written a play about five birds in a cage (*The Cagebirds*, 1971, one of his most successful) and I could hear this voice saying, "Oh, we've finished with birds, have we, and gone on to mice?"'

The idea for *Can You Hear The Music?* occurred when mice invaded David's loft ten years ago.

'It stayed as just an idea for quite a long time. I kept taking it out and looking at it and making odd little notes, some of them quite literally on the backs of envelopes, anything that floated across my mind that might well do for this particular idea.'

It wasn't until June 1987 that David began shaping his material into a play.

'At this stage I like to put down, in one sentence if I can, what the play is about. I've got to have a definite core before I can start setting it down in play form.'

The core will remain constant, but what David calls the 'decoration' – dialogue, characterisation, moves – will change during the writing and production.

'In this particular play I knew nothing about the characters when I started and let them establish themselves.

'To give you an example of how a play can change in the writing, my latest play, which is only in the manuscript stage at the moment, was to be about a party of youngsters finding one room in an empty house exactly as it had been in the mid-Edwardian era. That was my first thought, but when I started to write it turned out to be 1915 and a sort of ghost that takes over one of the youngsters was going to be a conscientious objector.

'When I had the play read at the Leicestershire Playwrights – we meet once a fortnight and read our plays to one another – they said it would be far stronger if, instead of someone just objecting on principle, it was an officer who had been in the war for three years and was not going back. So then I changed the time of the play from 1915 to 1917.'

David nearly always starts off his plays in longhand. 'At this stage I find it quicker. The longhand is my first draft; that gets edited and then I go to my typewriter.'

From there David goes to the Gestetner in his garage – 'If I were starting now it would be a photocopier,' he says – and turns out enough copies for reading, because it's now, at second draft stage, that he tries it out on other people.

'It's amazing the faults that reading aloud can reveal. For instance – just a little thing – I'll realise I've used a phrase three times already but it doesn't hit you till then. Also, you can get a better idea of the length. Nearly always I find a script reads longer than I thought it would.

'With *Can You Hear The Music?* there was a point where I was a bit stuck and one of the Leicestershire Playwrights said, "One of the mice would have to be left behind otherwise there would be no one to tell the story. She should be deaf, so she wouldn't be able to hear the Piper." Once I'd got that, it cleared quite a block from the play. One should never be afraid to take advice!'

In some parts of the country you may be lucky enough to find a group which has professional actors to read at manuscript stage. At one such group, connected with Leicester's Phoenix Theatre, an unknown writer, Sue Townsend, turned up with ten pages of writing and said, 'This is a something, but I don't really know what it is.'

David was one of the actors reading it. 'I didn't know what it was either, but I said, "If I were you I'd sent it to the BBC." It was, of course *Adrian Mole*; at the time of reading – Nigel Mole.'

David then amends the second draft and incorporates suggestions and ideas that have come out of the reading. Next he either finds an amateur group prepared to put it on, or goes for the more rarified atmosphere of the professional theatre.

'The market for amateur plays is ready and open,' says David. 'For years now the income from it has taken care of my bread and butter, with TV, radio and the professional theatre adding the jam.

'The main demand comes from the one-act drama festival. Usually the rules specify a length of not less than 20 minutes and not more than 40. The good all-female play is a most sought-after commodity. Settings requiring ingenuity and imagination, rather than a naturalistic domestic interior, are in demand. There is nothing quite so liberating to the dramatic imagination as an empty stage. Lighting should be simple, but costuming can be as elaborate as you please.'

David approached six amateur societies in Leicester before he found any takers for *Can You Hear The Music?* The most common complaint about it was – because at this point it had no stage directions – that it was too static. In the end he was only able to get it done by directing it himself.

A bit too much like vanity publishing? Not at all. David Campton is no tyro looking for his name in lights. He's a highly respected writer, actor and director who's written a play which – because it's a bit unusual – some groups are not prepared to tackle. Of course, at this stage even David can't be sure it will work, but the only way to find out is to get it put on.

David's faith was rewarded. The play came first in the Leicester and County One-Act Drama Festival. The adjudicator, Ian Bradley, had this to say about it: 'It offers tremendous scope for originality by designer, director and actors . . . an interpretation that had style, wit, contrast and a bravura approach.'

David finds that now there are surprisingly few taboos when writing for the stage, even for the amateur market. 'There,' he says, 'the main one is language, although that's easier than it used to be. The amateur theatre is now very catholic in its choice of plays – a look at what's being put on by local drama groups is a good guide. Orton, Ayckbourn, even Beckett is not unknown – but you do have to bear the type of audience in mind, and the number of characters, too.

'The optimum number of cast for a Women's Institute or Townswomen's Guild is six. More than that and they have difficulty finding performers. It's different if you're writing for a school, of course.'

An added advantage of an amateur production for a writer is that you can see where the play is sagging.

'During rehearsals of *Can You Hear The Music?* I put the blue pencil through whole chunks of the script. Another point is that professional performers can make even very bad writing work. If your amateur actors have trouble learning particular lines it's important for the writer to go back and look at them. The thought process is probably wrong and the author needs to make corrections before it goes any further.

'As well as suggesting the underlying thought process the dialogue must create atmosphere. It should never be just a medium for conveying information.'

After the Leicester Festival David typed the final draft of *Can You Hear The Music?*, amending anything he felt could be improved, adding all the moves from the production, plus a lighting plot and a list of props.

'I deliberately make my character outlines vague at this stage, then it opens up the possibilities for future productions. Of course, if there are some specific requirements for a character, I will state them.'

When everything was completed – 'The very best that I could make it,' says David – he sent the play to Samuel French for publication. Did he think they would take it?

'No. In fact, French's have turned down as many of mine as

they have published.' (In this instance, however, they have accepted the play for publication.)

'French's will publish a play that has not been produced, if they like it. It helps if it has been produced, and if it's gone on to receive a good adjudication in a festival or win an award, better still. Or if it's had a good notice in the local paper. It all helps.'

David advises you not to send a *long* letter about *yourself* when submitting your play. 'Let the play (and what's happened to it) speak for itself.' Should a play not be accepted by French's David will try another publisher. There's a list of play publishers in the *Writers' and Artists' Year Book*.

Don't be downhearted if a publisher does turn your play down. David's play *Cards, Cups and Crystal Ball*, about three incompetent fortune-tellers who suddenly find they're not as incompetent as they thought they were, was turned down by French's who said they already had a play about fortune-tellers.

This seemed to David a rather flimsy reason for rejecting it. 'However, some months after that it was broadcast on the radio, with Margaret Boyd, Pauline Letts and Rosemary Leach. I had a very good response to the play and a good notice in the *Telegraph*.'

French's then did an about-turn and published it, having been inundated with requests for amateur groups, who, of course, knew David's name and were most surprised to find that the play wasn't in print.

'Failing publication by someone like French's the only thing to do now is advertise your play – as I do – either in *Amateur Stage*, or if it's a play with an all-female cast, in *Home and Country* (the W.I. magazine) or *Townswoman*, and make sure you have sufficient copies to cover at least one application.

'I charge the same rate as French's,' says David. 'I have to avoid getting into collision with them. The same for royalties. The current fee for a one-act play is £12 plus VAT per performance.

'Whereas most full-length plays must have West End seal of approval before amateurs consider them acceptable, original one-act plays are accepted on their merits.

'I remember a Townswomen's Guild Drama Conference at which there were over 1,000 delegates; as another (now very successful) playwright murmured at the time, 'Think of a thousand performing fees.'

'Never turn down a commission, even from your local Youth Club, because you never know where it may lead. You never know who may come to see it, or what will develop from the production.'

Mary Rensten has written plays for the stage, both amateur and professional, and for radio. She has also written a non-fiction book and numerous feature articles for national magazines.

Writing a Pantomime

Jackie Short

Ever thought of writing a pantomime? Now is the time of year that amateur drama groups begin scouring French's catalogue for something suitable for a Christmas production. Many will be disappointed.

The problem is that most published pantos require a large cast, with a preponderance of men. Most local drama groups are small, with a preponderance of women. What they need is a competent writer who can tailor a pantomime story to their needs – i.e. YOU!

So, get to know your local players, see one of their performances to give you an idea of their strengths and weaknesses, and then offer your services.

Convincing them you are just what they want shouldn't be difficult – don't be offended by the odd, 'Er, um, no disrespect, but wouldn't we be safer with a *proper* panto?' Such is the veneration for the published word.

Point out that you may offer your script to Samuel French Ltd at some future date, so this is their chance to perform it before it attracts royalties. Besides, you will write it to their precise requirements. Watch their doubts fade.

Before you set pen to paper, have a good look at the stage they use. Unless they are very lucky, it'll be a dingy village hall with almost no back-stage room for set changes, nowhere to store flats, no revolving trap door in the stage for special effects. Probably there will be only rudimentary stage lighting and no sound system. (Can they obtain one? You need to know before you incorporate cannon fire, trumpet blasts and claps of thunder in your tale.)

Find out too about the availability of the stage. It's no use designing a wonderful set that takes three weeks to construct if they can only get onto the stage two days before the performance.

Now to your story line. Unless the group has a strong preference, why not avoid the exhausted tales of Cinderella and Jack and the Beanstalk? Be original so your pantomime stands out from the crowd. There are hundreds more fairy tales waiting for adaptation.

Remember the constitution of the group. If there are only three men, then have a heroine instead of a hero. If the princess rescues the prince, you can probably co-opt the good-looking assistant stage manager who can't act. Keep him locked in a tower by a wicked witch for most of the action and bring him out for the finale. You'll please all the mums and little girls in the audience – at last an active heroine! And many dads and little boys may be relieved that for once the Prince doesn't have to behave like Superman.

You may choose your story for originality, but exclude all the panto traditions at your peril! A panto without an ugly sister or dame played by a man is no panto. It's a perennial joke that all generations love.

Remember to write this part for the best and most masculine-looking actor in the group. It'll be the plum role and requires real acting skill to extract every ounce of humour from his ludicrous disguise.

And he must look ludicrous in women's clothes: the ambiguity of the drag artist is not right for panto. Panto demands the absurdity of the stubbly chin and hairy chest, knock-knees and hobnail boots, inadequately disguised as a woman.

Another popular role is that of the principal boy – a shapely, leggy lady in fishnet tights. She doesn't have to play the 'male' lead, you can make her a 'Buttons' type character if she can't sing, for instance, and you want the prince to sing. Remember, amateur theatricals are done for fun, but the performers are delicate blossoms and their egos are easily punctured. Know your cast and don't ask them to do anything they can't, though do stretch their talents – they'll love rising to a challenge.

This brings us to music. A panto needs songs. Find out what musical talents your group possesses. If you've a middle-aged banjo player, then incorporate this talent in his part. If the actress who's exactly right for the Wicked Queen has a wonderful voice, then give her most of the songs. Be flexible and know your cast.

Accompaniment can be a bugbear. If there is no pianist in the company, hiring one can be beyond the finances of many groups. Remember this when planning your songs. You can of course have a taped backing if there is a sound system to relay it.

When choosing songs, remember the laws governing performing rights. It's safer to stick to folk tunes which most people know, are easy to sing and easy to accompany, than risk using pop songs. Write your own words if the originals aren't suitable.

So, you've got your story, you know your cast's talents, now get writing the script. Rhyming couplets are an old pantomime tradition and recommended for amateur actors. You as the writer can have great fun with horribly contrived rhymes, and rhyme is much easier for the cast to learn than prose speeches. As humour is an essential part of a pantomime and hard to write, rhyming couplets give you a joke platform to spring from.

Don't forget the tradition of audience participation, a song perhaps, or the old. *'Oh yes, it is! Oh no, it isn't!'* routine.

Another source of humour is the local joke. Do make use of your local knowledge. Audiences love quips about local figures and institutions (non-libellous). Sometimes, generous shops will lend props and furniture in return for a 'plug' in your script – worth consideration.

You may be thinking, it sounds like a lot of hard work, so what's in it for me? The answer is a positive one: you'll get excellent practice at plotting, setting and characterisation. It will get your work known by a wide local audience and your local paper will almost certainly be interested in doing a feature on you. You'll have the pleasure of seeing your work performed, and that's a pleasure like no other, and finally, your work will give pleasure to a great many people.

Isn't that what writing's all about? Oh yes, it is!

Jackie Short is Principal of a Community Education Centre and writes in her spare time. She has had articles published in a variety of national and local magazines; she has written three so far unpublished novels, all of which she is still working on.

Oh No She Didn't!

Ann Stevens

When I was first asked to write a pantomime for my village Women's Institute, my immediate response was to refuse. After all, I couldn't write drama – repeated battering at the door of the BBC drama department had convinced me of that! And I had never seen a homespun local pantomime – I didn't know how these things were done. Finally, I was too busy. There were competitions to enter, I had a couple of articles in the pipeline and several stories buzzing round my head; not to mention my ongoing first novel.

But when I had had time to reflect, I realised I could be turning down an offer I really shouldn't refuse. Firstly, here was proof that I was being recognised as a writer in my little local community, flattering to my ego and a boost to my confidence. Secondly, since there was no editor to satisfy, there was no chance of my script being rejected – and my immortal words would be uttered for all to hear!

So I agreed, with one proviso – that I collaborate with another WI member who, I knew, had previous experience of such productions. Together, we arranged a meeting, to which we would come armed with 'ideas'!

As is the way with these things, once started the ideas flowed thick and fast. The only problem was to merge them into a composite whole without either of us giving – or taking – too much. Collaboration in creativity, I discovered, is not easy. I welcomed help in the sticky bits, but found it hard to subjugate my own ideas in favour of my colleague's. But since without her we would never have got started at all (she knew exactly the right note for the opening dialogue) I had to admit that I couldn't have done it without her.

We called our pantomime *Cinderella in Boots*, as I was particularly keen on the idea of merging several pantomime themes into one, with a lot of local colour thrown in for good measure. Our heroine was a milkmaid who lived in her muddy black boots and dreamed of 'green wellies', of going to all our familiar village activities and meeting a handsome 'prince'. Our hero was Jack, who lived on the new estate and grew a giant beanstalk whose beans won the village flower show, while Jack won dear Cinders' heart. The clock struck five and Cinders rushed to do her milking, leaving behind a Wellington boot which Jack rescued tenderly. This brought the house down on the night, and was followed by a wistful little song to the tune of 'I've Grown Accustomed to her Face'.

To my surprise I found I had quite a knack for writing songs to well-known tunes, and managed all eight of these to such old faithfuls as 'Some Day my Prince will Come' and 'Daisy, Daisy'. Our one expense was to hire Daisy – a big and beautiful Friesian cow costume with huge pink udders and an appealingly expressive face. She was the hit of the show – and gave it the professional touch we needed.

We cast our characters in June, gave out the scripts under strict orders of secrecy (especially about the cow!) and everyone went away to think about it until September.

The first rehearsal, in the rectory dining room, was depressing to say the least. The measurements of the village hall stage, carefully marked out on the carpet were constrictingly small. People had dropped out, our 'villagers' were dwindling and we only had half a cow. Somehow, the remaining cast stumbled through their lines, but stage directions which had flowed easily from the keys of my word processor proved almost impossible to execute, at least by amateurs who couldn't let go of their scripts.

Two months later they still couldn't let go of their scripts! My co-author/producer and I were in despair. After all, the whole thing ran for only an hour – it wasn't exactly *Gone with the Wind*. Was it too much to expect them to learn their words? Grudgingly, we had to be satisfied with a near-approximation to some of our carefully-crafted speeches, and in so doing learned a valuable lesson. It's one thing to write a play, quite another to produce it as well, when any insistence on accuracy and sticking to the script smacks of the worst sort of ego-trip on the part of the authors.

However, what they missed out in accuracy, the cast more than made up for in enthusiasm. By December, everyone had worked out and acquired an appropriate costume; in some cases, several, necessitating breathless changes in the cramped kitchen off the stage. The Ugly Sisters sported monstrous turquoise and purple wigs, huge busts and horrendous make-up and had devised a funny dance routine. The 'Rector' had adopted some familiar mannerisms and in so doing had enlarged on his part admirably. Props were made and collected; a pianist co-opted for the occasion had worked hard with the singers, going over and over the songs, getting the timing right, and someone had even produced a microphone and amplifier which meant we could hear the frailest singing voice at the back of the hall.

Meanwhile, dry rot had been discovered in the stage, which threatened imminent collapse! Before we could use it, it had to be removed and completely rebuilt by two skilled, loyal and hardworking husbands. At the same time it was enlarged, the single overhead bulb replaced by spots – and then, hey presto, we even had flootlights, and scenery.

Two weeks before P-day the whole thing suddenly exploded into life. On the new enlarged stage and in the glow of the footlights, people actually began to enjoy themselves. Scripts were finally abandoned and props were used freely and naturally. In my prompt corner in front of the stage – from where I also operated one of the curtains and led the audience participation, I anxiously followed each line of 'my' script, willing them all at least not to leave anything out, timing the whole thing carefully. One hour exactly, including four scene changes, with room for a few encores and an extra laugh or two. I began to relax – and enjoy myself too.

And then it was the big night, when we performed to the WI Christmas Party. We knew it would go down well as we had included so many local characters – in the nicest possible way – and lots of village activities. And we weren't disappointed. But the following night, when we packed one hundred friends and neighbours into the village hall and it was standing room only, was the best of all. To hear so many people laughing at our jokes, singing along with our songs, booing and aahing and applauding, was quite the biggest buzz I have had from my writing career so far.

And when at the end someone shouted 'author, author', and we were both presented with enormous bouquets, well . . . we just can't wait to start again on next year's production – *Dick Whittington's Goose* maybe?

Ann Stevens has made a good start to her writing career. In her first three years she has sold more than two dozen short stories and a variety of articles to magazines. She has written two (so far unpublished) novels and a serial for a women's magazine – and won several prizes in short-story competitions.

Creating Landscapes in the Mind

Bill Bradley

For anyone with ambitions to write a play, national radio is the medium in which success is most likely to be achieved.

Compared with television and the stage, a radio play is cheap to produce, and this is the main reason why the BBC is able to take the risk of using previously unknown writers. Every year 60 or 70 writers, whose works have never been published or performed before, succeed in having a radio play performed.

There is a high turnover of dramatic work on national radio. During a sample four-week period the BBC broadcast 42 plays, 11 of them on Radio 3 and 31 on Radio 4. Thirteen of them had repeat broadcasts. Twenty different directors and 37 different authors were involved in the production of the 42 plays.

Adaptations of works by Conan Doyle and Virginia Woolf, and a translation of Victor Hugo's work were included in the sample period, but they were only a minor proportion. The names of many of the writers would be unfamiliar to most people, but so were the names of Harold Pinter and Tom Stoppard when they first appeared in the *Radio Times*.

Unfortunately local radio has not followed in the footsteps of its national big brother, no doubt because of the strict financial limitations imposed on the local stations.

The first thing the radio (or any other) dramatist needs is something to say. The average audience for *Saturday Night Theatre*, with its repeat on Monday afternoon, is well over one million. These listeners set aside up to an hour and a half of their time and make the extra effort required to follow a radio play. They need to be convinced that it was worthwhile. So although the opportunities are there for the writer, no one should think that just anything will do.

There are a number of regular categories of plays which follow a set pattern. *Drama Now*, *The Friday Play* and *Studio 3*, which are broadcast on Radio 3, are usually experimental or classical works.

Plays which have a more general and popular appeal come out on Radio 4. These include *Saturday Night Theatre*, *The Late Play* and batches of shorter plays such as *Tales Out Of School* and *Fear on Four*.

A would-be writer is well advised to study the different categories and decide which of them would make the best vehicle for whatever it is he/she wants to write.

Because of programming planning requirements most radio plays are either 30, 60 or 90 minutes in length. Twenty-six of the 42 plays broadcast in the sample four weeks were written to these precise timings.

But there were also plays broadcast of 32, 35, 40, 45, 47 and 75 minutes duration. There was even one on Radio 3 which ran for 125 minutes. And although the new writer would be wise to confine himself to 30, 60 or 90 minutes if possible, this should not be looked on as a strict, unbreakable rule.

Having decided on what it is he/she wants to say, the playwright must decide who is going to say it. Characterisation is just as important in a radio play as in any other form of fictional work, perhaps even more so. There is no opportunity to use facial expressions or gestures as on the stage, or the TV screen; no means of describing a character in the way it can be done in a short story or a novel. The characters have to convey their personalities, their moods and their attitudes to the listener by the words they speak and the way they speak them.

It is important therefore, that the radio playwright gets to know the characters thoroughly; that they are alive in the mind when writing dialogue. Otherwise they will not come to life in the mind of the listener.

Each character should have an individual way of using words so that the listener will be able to distinguish one from the other, not just because the actors' voices are different, but also because of the different ways in which the characters put words together. One could be loquacious, another taciturn, another abrupt, another meek or shy. These characteristics should be apparent from the written words before the actor puts his/her own interpretation on them.

It is always worthwhile for a writer to read dialogue out loud, simultaneously visualising the character who is speaking and checking the resonance and credibility of the words coming from the lips of the character which has been created.

Having thought of an original idea for a play, the writer will no doubt have some idea of how the story will unfold. Supporting the theory that anything benefits from being planned, it is usually worthwhile to write a preliminary summary (synopsis) of the storyline, perhaps in scenes, perhaps as rough notes, perhaps as a continuous narrative. This will give an opportunity to check that the completed play will be balanced and presented in such a way that the listener's interest will be grasped in the early stages and will be maintained throughout.

As the actual playwriting proceeds and the characters develop more fully in the writer's mind, better ideas may emerge. It might also occur that the characters themselves will suggest other courses of action, or will not fit satisfactorily in with what has been planned for them. A particular course of action may not comply with that character's personality or mood at that specific point in the play.

Writers who are new to radio can sometimes worry too much about how they present and set out their work. There is a standard format. A specimen page is included in the book issued by BBC Publications, *Writing For The BBC*. At a talk given recently by Dave Sheasby, one of the BBC's regional drama producers, he warned new writers against being obsessed by this.

All scripts should be neatly typed, with generous margins. The characters' names should be shown on the left-hand side against each speech and the speech should begin about one third of the way across the page. Sound effects should be on a separate line with double line spacing between each speech and/or sound effect.

If the play is accepted, copies will be typed out by the BBC, set out in the form required with numbered speeches, detailed sound effects, the required brackets, underlinings, use of capital letters and so on, which each have their own significance to the production team.

It is a mistake to tell the actors how to deliver their words by using directions in brackets such as:

SUSAN (ANGRILY)   Don't you dare!

The 'angrily' is not needed because the mood is expressed in the words themselves and the actor will interpret them accordingly.

Elaborate definition of sound effects should also be avoided. The words (<u>CAR ARRIVING</u>) are quite sufficient. There is no need to write:

(CRUNCH OF TYRES ON GRAVEL. CAR ENGINE NOISE. ENGINE NOISE DIES. DOOR OPENS. FOOTSTEPS ON GRAVEL. CAR DOOR CLOSES.)

Filling in such detail is the job of the sound effects engineer. He/she will do it much more professionally than any writer could do.

The same advice applies to background music. This is something usually best left to the producer or director unless the writer has a piece of music in mind which has special significance for the characters and is an essential element of the play.

Writing and producing a radio play is a team job. A writer needs to remember that other members of the team will want to play their part and will not necessarily welcome someone else trying to do it for them. The director, the producer, the actors, the sound effects person and other technicians, all have a contribution to make and they will all be experts in their own field.

Dave Sheasby was asked what qualities he looks for in a MS. His reply was that he looks for content, for something being said, for a statement. He also emphasised the importance of distinct characters and realistic dialogue.

He advised new writers to 'be their own person', not to imitate, to be original, to write what they wanted to write not what they think the BBC wants. Dave stressed the huge potential of the radio play, its ability to create 'landscapes in the mind'. And he urged new writers to take advantage of this facility to create images in the minds of the listeners.

The best way for a writer to 'get the feel' of how a radio play works is to listen to as many of them as possible, to tape them and listen again. Discover how the play is structured, how the characters are created and displayed, how information is presented to the listener without making it obvious that that is what is being done.

Some radio plays have been printed in book form and can be borrowed from libraries. This presents another opportunity for detailed study. There are also books on the subject of radio playwriting. Two of the most useful ones are *Writing For The BBC* and *The Way To Write Radio Drama* by William Ash, who was a script editor in the BBC radio drama department for 15 years. A pamphlet *Notes on Radio Drama* will be supplied by the script unit on request.

The completed play can be submitted either to the Radio Drama Script Unit or to one of the regional offices at Leeds, Birmingham, Manchester, Bristol, Edinburgh, Cardiff or Belfast.

If a writer feels that his/her play is the sort of work usually handled by a particular director, it is acceptable for the play to be submitted directly to that person. This of course can be established only by listening to plays directed by him/her. The directors' names are included in the credits listed in the *Radio Times* as well as being mentioned at the time the play is broadcast.

There are between 30 and 40 people involved in reading plays which are submitted to the BBC. They are all read and judged on their merits.

If a play is accepted the writer will usually be invited to a discussion before production work begins, and may be invited to rehearsals. Production is quite quick, rarely more than four days. A half-hour play will be produced in one day. Usually about nine months elapse between production and broadcast. Professional actors are always used and a writer may even be fortunate enough to have a big name speak the words he/she has written.

Success in radio can often lead to success in other areas of writing. Stage and television are geared to writers with established 'track records'. Radio can be a way of achieving this.

Fees are smaller than those paid for television but are not insignificant. Rates are on a 'per minute' basis, with a lower rate for beginners than for established writers. In his book, William Ash states that in 1984 the writer of a 90 minute play, with a repeat, could expect to receive about £3,000. In 1989, the Writers' Guild told WM that a first-time BBC radio drama script writer would be paid £15.95 per minute.

The Joke's on You

Jim Eldridge

Writing comedy for television and radio falls into two categories: character comedy and joke comedy. Briefly, joke comedy is the sort you find in sketch shows such as *The Two Ronnies*, *Spitting Image*, *Weekending*, etc., where the point is to create a short sketch with a funny tag. I worked in this genre during the early 70s on a variety of shows, mainly for Radio 2 and Radio 4, and found it a hard taskmaster/mistress for the following reasons:

1. You have to be funny for the whole duration of the sketch, you cannot allow pauses for 'reflective thought'.

2. If you are to earn a decent living then you have to produce many, many such sketches. This is because comedy writers are paid per minute of broadcast material, and no one can exist on the money they would get for two or three minutes worth of material per week.

3. On a comedy sketch show like Radio 4's *Weekending*, each writer is in competition with loads of others to get his/her sketch accepted.

Because of this, the vast majority of sketch/gag writers tend to be highly stressed, underpaid individuals desperate to find a joke, or a punch-line, in anything. Is such stress worth it financially? Yes, if you make the top league, of which just a small handful in this country do. However, for me the answer was a resounding NO.

This brings me to the other branch of comedy: character comedy, more popularly known as 'sitcom'. Even here there are two divisions: sitcom played before a TV or radio audience (eg 'Allo 'Allo; *Up the Elephant and Round the Castle*, etc.) and TV or radio comedy made *without* an audience (eg *MASH*, my own *King Street Junior*, etc.). As a writer who has worked in both, my preference is for the second style (non-audience). However, in this article I intend to outline the problems and advantages of both methods as a guide to those who wish to write TV or radio sitcom.

Audience shows

As its name suggests, this sort of show is recorded before a live audience. This immediately presents you with the following problems when constructing a script:

1. The half-hour script must be confined to a few studio sets so that it can be recorded within a certain allotted space of time (e.g. 90 minutes).

2. The purpose of making a sitcom in front of a live audience is so that the listeners or viewers at home can hear the studio audience laughing. This is because many of the powers-that-be believe that the audience at home won't realise that they are watching or listening to a comedy programme unless they can hear audience laughter.

An interesting example of this is the American comedy series *MASH*. Although this series was recorded without a live audience, in America it is shown with a 'laugh track' (i.e. a soundtrack of dubbed-on audience laughter at the funny bits) on it. It was offered to the BBC 'with or without laugh track'. Fortunately, in my opinion, the BBC bought it without.

To make the live audience laugh the script must have lots of obvious jokes in it. As has been pointed out to me on various occasions, 'the audience at home cannot hear the live audience if they smile. We have to make them *laugh*'.

As an added insurance, a 'warm-up man' will often cajole the studio audience into laughing. If they haven't laughed loud enough the warm-up man will actually conduct the audience into laughing at it. The result of this is too often laughter that sounds faked.

A further problem with this set-up is that some actors play to the live audience, rather than to the camera (and the audience at home). This can make the character that actor is playing less believable to the audience at home.

Having made all these negative points, the positive point is that writing and making sitcoms in this way can be a lot of fun (as well as very lucrative if it becomes popular).

3. The show has to be recorded in chronological order (i.e. it has to be 'played' as a comedy play, in the right order – rather than the method used in film-making, where scenes are shot out of sequence for greater efficiency).

Non-audience shows
1. The great advantage in my opinion is that the script can afford to be subtle and raise a smile in the audience and does not need to have constant 'gut-busters'.
2. Moments of drama can be injected into the show, making the situation more 'real' than is permissible in most sitcoms. (Having said that, a great writer like John Sullivan is able to bring tender moments into the live-audience *Only Fools and Horses* very successfully.)
3. Recording and rehearsal time are combined during one whole day's recording, rather than the actual recording being stuck at the end of a day's run-throughs. This means that a scene that demands more time spent on it than other scenes can get that time, without having the studio audience getting fidgety.

In summing up I believe that the major difference between these two forms, audience and non-audience, is that the audience show is aimed primarily at the audience in the studio, whereas we should be writing comedy primarily for the TV and radio audience at home. (Having said all that, my own favourite TV comedy show is *Fawlty Towers*, a live-audience show.)

The technique of writing comedy
Having discussed all the above, which any writer of TV and radio sitcom needs to be aware of, what about the actual technique of writing comedy? How do you make people laugh out loud?

The answer to that, I'm afraid, is the same as to 'How long is a piece of string?' It depends. In this case it depends on the different types of audience: the comedian Bernard Manning may go down a storm in a northern club, but put him before a group of nuns and I doubt if he would be very well received.

Rule 1
Identify the audience you are aiming your comedy at. The wider that audience, the more successful your programme will be. (*Up The Elephant and Round The Castle*, for example, had an audience in the UK of 17 million. Compare that with a late-night alternative show which may have an audience of about one million.)

However, there are no guarantees that a 'broader' show will be more successful than one considered 'minority'. *Fawlty Towers*, for example, was given a BBC2 slot because it was considered 'minority taste' and 'not popular' enough for an airing on BBC1!

Really, the best rule in writing comedy (as with all writing) is: write to entertain yourself and your friends. After all, if you don't find something funny, why should you think anyone else will?

Rule 2

Humour should come from the characters. Often a line may appear completely unfunny on the printed page of the script, but put into the right mouth (eg Del Boy of *Only Fools and Horses*, Captain Mainwaring of *Dad's Army*, Audrey of *To The Manor Born*, etc) and even the word 'Oh?' can raise gales of laughter.

Developing the right characters does not come easily, it means a lot of observation of people in society. Who do you find funny in your circle of friends (and I do not mean 'funny' as in someone who can tell amusing anecdotes). Ask yourself: why is that person a great character – then reproduce that character (or parts of him/her) into a character of your own creation. This is the way that great comic creations are born. They are based largely on real people the author has known.

Rule 3

Choose a situation to set your character in. Choose one that you know about. This does not mean that you will need to have had actual experience of it (after all, Ben Elton and Richard Curtis didn't need to live in eighteenth-century England to write *Blackadder II*). But you should have complete knowledge of the situation you are writing about, you will be able to write about it more convincingly.

So: real characters in a believable setting.

Next: **Comedy business**, the parts (in addition to the comedy of character) that make people laugh.

Slapstick

Always gets a laugh, and has done ever since Ug the caveman bashed Og the caveman in the face with a brontosaurus pie. However, make sure that your visual slapstick suggestions are possible in the confines of the studio (ie that space and studio time permit).

When I was first writing TV comedy, in one show I did I wrote in a visual gag that required an actor to hurtle through a large window, shattering the glass. It took two hours for the special effects team to set up the window in such a way that it would collapse on impact.

We were doing it before a studio audience, which meant that the gag had to be done in one take; if the actor missed the window, or the window collapsed before he hit it, or one of the 10 million other things went wrong, then the shot would have been ruined.

Because of studio time limitations it would have been impossible to remount the shot. As this gag was the tag for the whole show, had it failed to work, the whole show would have been ruined.

Luckily for us, everything went okay on the night. But after 20 years in TV and radio I now realise that the number one rule, when actually in production, is Sod's Law: if it can go wrong, it will go wrong.

Dialogue

As I said earlier, dialogue that sounds funny does not always look funny on the page. And vice versa: many scripts that appear hilarious on the printed page are not so funny when the actors actually play the lines.

This is often because some new scriptwriters are still writing in a literary fashion rather than in an oral one. Lines of dialogue are meant to be spoken, not read.

New comedy scriptwriters should always try their scripts out by reading them aloud to a try-out audience (eg your long-suffering family). If you need to explain to them why a line is funny then it isn't funny, so cut it out.

Use jokes by all means, everybody does, but make the joke fit the character who is telling it. If a line is out of character then that character becomes implausible to the audience.

Plot

In my opinion a strong plot and one or two strong sub-plots within a half-hour sitcom are very important. However, that is my style, and I'd be the first to agree that there have been some brilliant comedy shows with no plot at all, such as Tony Hancock's *The Bedsitter*.

The reason why I like to have a strong plot is very simple: if the laugh lines flag a little, then at least you've got a strong story line to keep the audience interested and stop them switching over to another channel.

Influences
This is another word for 'stealing ideas'. People always ask me 'where do you get your ideas from?' The answers are: a) observing real life; b) watching and listening to comedy classics such as Laurel and Hardy, Jacques Tati, etc, and reworking a comedy routine. (After all, they got their routines from watching music hall artistes of their time. Some of the best routines are centuries old.)

Put all of these ingredients together, add an awful lot of perspiration from your brow, and (with a bit of luck) you'll have a comedy script that'll make you laugh. All you have to do now is persuade the powers-that-be in TV or radio that it'll make millions of other people laugh. But that's another story.

Jim Eldridge has been a professional writer for over 20 years. His credits as creator and writer include the award-winning BBC TV series Bad Boyes, *BBC radio's* King Street Junior, *and Thames TV's* Up the Elephant and Round the Castle. *He is also the author, with his son Duncan, of the best-selling series of books,* How to Handle Grown-Ups.

Getting a Book of Poems Published

Glyn Maxwell

One August morning, I got *The Letter*. As this is a writers' magazine, I don't think I need explain further, but yes it *is* worth the effort, and it sure beats the daydreams.

My first poem had been accepted exactly three years earlier, and the strangled yelp with which I absorbed that news had, over the course of much magazine publication, diminished to a mere smile.

But a good publisher's blessing on a whole book brought forth the squeals anew, and so I want to give some advice to anybody who wishes to open the mail one fine morning and lose the facility of coherent speech. There are no short cuts in this business, but there are ground rules and wrong ways of doing things. Nobody without talent is going to sneak into print – and be paid for it – but a good few deserving cases are bound to be hampering themselves in various ways.

I should know. I was the teenage poet sitting in a wood sulking because I wasn't well known, *before I'd sent a single poem anywhere*. I've since met others.

At the outset, let me apologise to those who feel that some of what I say is obvious or self-evident. Anyone who's met any magazine editors, 'readers' or publishers, or happens to be one, will agree that it isn't. And the precious commodity missing from most poetry – sense – is also most lacking in poets' attempts to see their work in print.

But I'll begin with an essential assurance: good poetry does rise to the top (whatever comes up with it); either quickly, in about one percent of cases; slowly, if you're lucky and can learn; or terribly slowly, the usual procedure.

Now here comes the obvious: the more you *read*, the more you *write*, and the more you *send out*, the quicker the process will be. If you slacken in any of these three things, it will take more time. You must be a poet, yes, but a student of poetry also, and a self-employed businessman licking envelopes and stamping return-addresses. (Unless you want to be 'discovered', in which case my only advice is to wrap up warm.)

By far the commonest way into the poetry scene is magazine publication. There is absolutely no point in submitting MSS to publishing houses without having had at least a few poems printed in reputable journals. The poet Peter Levi told me he'd had about a half-dozen poems in print before his first book was accepted. It took me nearly 30, which is probably closer to the average. The point is, one has to build up a reputation: the *Times Literary Supplement*, the *London Magazine*, the *London Review of Books*, *Poetry Review* and the best of the regional publications – these are what the poetry publishers read.

So, send your work to magazines, regularly, efficiently, and coldly: this is the business side of things. It is worth remembering that on this side your own opinion of your talent is an irrelevance. Stay businesslike or get hurt.

Begin by choosing, say, six magazines, perhaps two prestigious national ones, and four smaller, regional, publications. Send six poems to each of these. (Don't have the same poem 'out' in two places at once, as this can really antagonise editors, but turn this limit to your advantage: write more, so you have more to send.)

Treat this multiple submission as your first move in a long campaign – not as a whim or an off-chance. Oh, and don't talk about it. It's *your* campaign. Everybody to whom you mention it will later be at liberty to ask you what happened, and you'll probably have to admit that the poems were rejected. As a campaign, your submission must be well-orchestrated. Send all the poems on the same day. Write down which poems you sent, and where you sent them.

And now for some very basic, but extremely important, reminders. Send saes. Type the poems well, centre them on the page. Photocopy them, send the copies, and keep the originals: that way you hang on to the signs of Tipp-Ex and the magazine gets the clean sheets.

If you word-process the poems, do it to 'letter' quality; that is, not dot-matrix, and don't send those sheets with holes down both sides. They give the impression one is prouder of the technology than of the poem. Each poem should be on a separate page. No poem should exceed two pages: you're really lessening your chances. Remember, I'm talking about the very beginning of your poetic career, when it's their call, not yours.

There is no point in writing a long covering letter, ever. Yes, if you've been published elsewhere, mention that; (poetry editors *are* prepared, in general, to make allowances for differences in taste: '*I'm* not sure, but if so-and-so printed him, well maybe yes . . .': at least this editor will give your poems a bit more time) and be courteous. Not only does it do no good to refer to the poems, explaining or elucidating or apologising, but it can easily do harm.

If you try to speak for the poems, you are implying that they *need* help – which they shouldn't – they should speak for themselves. Furthermore, the editor or sub-editor will immediately realize that you don't get this point, that you don't understand the terms of your relationship with any potential publisher. Let's not forget, the unpublished poet could be a future giant, but as he's *unpublished*, he's a very junior partner.

Feeling and emotion belong in the poems, not in the acts of sending out and getting back. It is very important not to allow impatience or jealousy to pollute one's perspective. Poetry editors print work they like, not people they like.

If cliques develop, and they do, they do at least have an artistic base, broadly speaking – not a personal one, which is a lot more than can be said for most other professions. So there's no point in getting paranoid about the same names always appearing, and not yours – generally those people are there for the right reasons, and they're building reputations just like you want to: so get yourself among them.

Don't be depressed by the thousands of scribblers out there: you are one of them, your scribbling is depressing them. So scribble more, read more, send more. And when your poems are 'out in the field', *forget them.* They're on their own. Write new ones. *Practise.*

You're the new Keats, perhaps, the new Larkin, another Plath: well, your first batch will probably all be rejected, some very quickly. Now comes the most dangerous moment of your poetic career. Hold that rejection slip in your hand and look at it. I know people who lost it at this moment, or ceased to care, or got comfortably cynical. And I know of people who plaster their walls with the things.

Well, don't. If it's a flat rejection, a form-letter, chuck it in the bin and forget about it. (If it's encouraging at all, file it away for when you need that kind of encouragement.) You *mustn't* react emotionally, but it's important to *respond*, to turn the pain into advantage. Yes, you can suffer, you're bound to, but there are ways to suffer.

You can fume, 'They're wrong!' or 'I'm awful!' – you could be right on both or either count – but the fact is, *it doesn't matter*. Your poems are rejected, you can't change that, so change something else! Every time your poems come back, respond in the same way: read the Greats. It doesn't matter if you write sonnets, lyrics, epics, limericks, rap or dub – Shakespeare, Keats, Hardy, Frost, Auden did it all better than you can, so get them into your room and *let them teach*.

There is plenty of time and room for pride or arrogance in a poet's life, but it must always be perfectly equalled by humility and a lifelong willingness to learn from masters.

There are other things you can do if you have no books to hand: write a better poem than the poem just rejected. You won't want to, it will sting. Or look at one of the rejected poems. Make seven improvements. Or, if you have new poems ready, not yet 'out in the field', send them out.

If you stop sending poems, you are, to all intents and purposes, giving up. I sent batches of 20–30 out every six months or so. The first batch was turned down flat. The second yielded two acceptances; the third, seven, and I was on my way. What if I'd given up after the first, hurtful 'duck'?

Don't start blaming editors' apparent predilections – 'Oh, he hates rhyme,' or 'I'm too avant-garde for them,' – again, you may be right, but it's just as likely that you're not quite ready. A good poem is a good poem, whether rhymed, free, 'modern', formal, light: any editor who doesn't believe this isn't really worth his or her job.

It's a good idea to have a constant number of Things To Hope For; say, five. You could submit to three magazines and enter two competitions. When you don't win the prize, choose another magazine; when those poems come back, find a competition. Don't pin your hopes on one thing. In sport that's fine; in creative art it's looking for trouble. That goes for Nobel nominees as well as unknown poets.

As to which magazines to try, I can't improve on Vol. 3/6 and 7 of *Writers' Monthly*, Joyce Schreibman's survey. Failing that, the *Writers' And Artists' Yearbook* is essential: it lists them all. Most editors advise you to study the magazine first. If you can't afford to subscribe to too many, just take a look at them; large (especially university-town) bookshops usually stock them, and your best bet in London is probably the Poetry Library at the Royal Festival Hall. Take a notebook, jot things down.

Some general advice about keeping your output *organised*: always know these things about each poem: its name, its date of writing, who's rejected it so far, and which magazine it's with now. Keep tabs on your poems. After you've written a few, say, 30, start to assemble an elite, a First Division, those 15 or 20 you are sure are better than the rest. And keep that number constant.

When you write a poem good enough for your elite, relegate another to give it room. This elite will become the nucleus of an MS to send to publishers. Those poems outside the elite, I would sideline, or revise, or pillage for a good phrase or two, or destroy. Don't get attached. (I'm still learning this: I witnessed the poet Derek Walcott trashing – literally – a poem I'd already had published in a British magazine!)

Having had some magazine publication, it's time to assemble a publishable MS. Send 40 poems or so, in a coherent order, with a title. Don't skimp on presentation. Unless you're very well established in the magazines, getting a book taken is going to be harder than getting odd poems accepted – so don't worry about sending the same MS to various houses: the odds against a Double Yes are enormous.

Two of the most prestigious houses, Faber & Faber and Chatto & Windus, publish introductory anthologies every two years or so, 5–7 new poets in one book. Anyone under 30 should be trying for an Eric Gregory Award every year: the reward is money and recognition. (See the poetry magazines for details.)

And remember the small presses: some are excellent; check them out first. BUT – and it has to be said again and again – *don't ever pay to see your work in print*. It might look glorious and be very satisfying, but all it tells the world is that no one but you is prepared to pay to publish your work, and that you're now a little poorer than you were. And few, if any, will review the book – though that might be a good thing.

There is no reason whatever not to enter for competitions. If you win nothing, so what? Neither did hundreds of others. If you do win, the rewards can be enormous; winning a national prize can knock five or ten years off how long it might otherwise have taken to get a book published. It can make you well known, it can pay a few bills.

To sum up, if you want a book of poems published, you have to get into the magazines (unless you're one of the blessed who wins prizes). To do so, you have to send, take rejection, send again, and keep sending. To give up disheartens only one's self. To be rejected is as much a part of the poet's life as buying stationery, or feeling good about the one you just wrote, or, one fine day, picking up that envelope that has no rejected poems in it, just a little note from the publisher. Good luck.

Glyn Maxwell was born in Hertfordshire; he went to Oxford University and Boston – where he worked with the poet Derek Walcott. He works as a freelance editor and reviewer (for TLS, *etc.). His first poetry collection,* Tale of the Mayor's Son, *was published by Bloodaxe in 1990; it won the Poetry Book Society Choice and is shortlisted for the John Llewellyn Rhys Prize.*

4

WRITING STYLE

Whatever you write, be it fiction or non-fiction, drama or verse, there is one essential. As the popular song says, 'You've gotta have . . . style.'

But what is style? Writing style is . . . really, whatever *works*. A writer may adjust his/her style to the needs of a particular project, but the basic, underlying style is likely to remain. It is likely that each writer's style is unique to each individual.

That said, there are aspects of style that can be adjusted – improved even. We can all learn to write better, to pick up points of technique. And that is what this section of the book is about – aspects of writing technique.

The two articles in this section are both by Jim McIntosh – poet, article writer, teacher and . . . enthusiast. He is even enthusiastic about writing style and techniques.

The first article, 'Do You Mean That Literally?' looks at the use and abuse of the metaphor. The second, 'Strictures on Structure', reviews three different ways of handling an interview – and cleverly incorporates a lot of interesting and motivating information about best-selling author Jessica Stirling.

Do You Mean That Literally?

Jim McIntosh

Rosalind said, 'Men are April when they woo, December when they wed.'
 I thought, 'Nice. Nicely put'.
 What was so good about it?
 The metaphor.
 Although many people might not know precisely why some people's talk is so striking or attractive, and still fewer would be able to recognise a metaphor as such (far less define what a metaphor is), I think it is true that metaphor is one of the major elements at the heart of striking speech or writing.
 Just look at that last sentence: 'At the heart of' – a metaphor. Even 'striking' has a metaphorical trace in it, though in this case it is something of a 'dead' metaphor (which is a metaphor, of course).
 Keats asserted that 'poetry is vitally metaphorical', and Aristotle argued that metaphor was not only a sign of intellectual superiority, but that it couldn't be taught, in the sense that you either had a gift for metaphor or you didn't.
 Some language theorists, I believe, consider that the metaphors we use actually help shape our attitudes to the world around us. For example, think of some of the metaphors we regularly employ when dealing with argument:
 We 'take sides', we 'defeat' our opponents, we 'withdraw' from a 'position', we 'concede defeat', we 'marshal our arguments', we 'win a victory', we 'pierce' our enemy's 'defences'.
 The whole thing is conceived as an aggressive procedure, not co-operative, not a combined seeking after truth, not a friendly or mutually beneficial endeavour. Could it be that we might have had better results if the metaphorical language applied to argument were selected from a different range or field or vocabulary?
 Anyway, it is quite incontrovertible that metaphor is almost always essential to good writing, in poetry or prose. So it is a subject well worth our studying.

Let's clear out of the way what a metaphor is. Here is how we were taught the subject at school (and I supply the very examples we were supplied with): 'A metaphor is a figure of speech in which one thing is identified with another, e.g. "He was a lion in the fight." '; 'A simile is a figure of speech in which one thing is said to be like another, and is usually shown by the words "like" and "as", as in "He was like a lion in the fight." '

We would then mark the similes/metaphors in a whole string of sentences deliberately calculated to demonstrate them.

Such exercises produced little understanding.

I think it might be more valuable to think of it this way:

Suppose you had a foreigner who had a grasp of English, but only a partial grasp. He might hear someone say, for instance, 'Do you see that talkative youngster over there? Wow, he's so dumb', or, 'That thin student is so thick'. The listener might understandably be puzzled by these apparently self-contradictory comments.

What he hasn't realised at that point is that in each sentence one of the adjectives (eg 'talkative') is meant literally, and the other (eg 'dumb') is meant 'metaphorically' or (a wider sense) 'figuratively'. The speaker intends a secondary meaning for the word.

The distinction between literal and metaphorical is one of the absolutely fundamental ones in language. And even if the non-literary citizen might not be able to explain it, it is one he nevertheless observes in his everyday speech and reading/writing.

Consider all of these expressions from normal conversational English: 'She has a really sharp tongue'; 'the remark was too pointed to ignore'; 'I'm totally broken-hearted'; 'I've a load on my mind'; 'her eyes were like stars'; 'the economic burden is crushing our country'; 'keep your head and you'll land on your feet'; 'my tongue felt furry'; 'I know what side my bread's buttered on'; 'I hung on every word she said'.

I've deliberately selected in the foregoing list expressions which are generally so common that they have lost much of their freshness – so much so that we hardly recognize them as metaphorical. These are what are known as dead metaphors.

Unless you are after a particular effect, it is advisable to avoid dead metaphors in your writing.

But when you examine good writing, you will find that the

better writers use metaphor, or figurative language generally, with originality or freshness, especially in poetry.

Let's look at some examples:

'The moon was a ghostly galleon tossed upon cloudy seas', (A. Noyes). 'The Assyrian came down like a wolf on the fold', (Byron). 'Life's but a walking shadow, a poor player, that struts and frets his hour upon the stage', (Shakespeare). 'Life, like a dome of many-coloured glass, Stains the white radiance of Eternity, Until Death comes and tramples it to fragments', (Shelley). 'I fall upon the thorns of life, I bleed', (Shelley). 'And from the craggy ledge the poppy hangs in sleep', (Tennyson).

You can see that sometimes the metaphor is a straight claim that one thing *is* another, as in 'Life's but a . . .'; sometimes it consists in attributing human attributes to non-human things (as in the poppy 'hangs in sleep'), in which instance it is sometimes referred to as 'personification'; sometimes the metaphorical idea is conveyed by 'like', as in 'like a wolf . . .'

Again, even one word can carry metaphorical implications, as in 'The smouldering sun . . .'

I suppose it is common to consider metaphor in poetry primarily, mainly because it is a device that poets have used with great effect. And generally speaking, metaphors can be more striking and original given a poetic context. You can get away with more in poetry, not in the sense of the poet being indulgent, but simply that the very appearance of verse on the page sets up certain expectations in the reader.

The reader is ready to go along with certain things, such as repetition and rhythmical effects, and rhyme, perhaps, and more adventurous language – including metaphorical language. So, let us stay with poetic metaphor a little longer.

Sometimes, a metaphor can extend throughout a whole poem, giving what is being said a richer impact. One example of this is in Roger McGough's poem, 'Fight of the Year', where the succeeding seasons of the year are seen as fighting a boxing-match with one another, with winter inevitably losing to spring.

One part of the poem is presented as a referee's counting-out of a fallen fighter, like this:

'1 tomatoes
2 radish

3 cucumber
4 onions
5 beetroot
6 celery
7 and any
8 amount
9 of lettuce
10 for dinner
Winter's out for the count
Spring is the winner!'

In older poetry, particularly epic poetry, poets often employed what they called 'Homeric simile', where the simile was much more detailed and elaborate than normal, as in this example from Matthew Arnold's 'Sohrab and Rustum' (at the point where the father, in ignorance, beholds his young warrior son):

'As some rich woman, on a winter's morn,
Eyes through her silken curtains the poor drudge
Who with numb blacken'd fingers makes her fire –
At cock-crow, on a starlit winter's morn,
When the frost flowers the whiten'd window panes –
And wonders how she lives, and what the thoughts
Of that poor drudge may be; Rustum ey'd
The unknown adventurous youth . . .'

You can see the heightened effect this kind of writing gives, especially in a long, descriptive poem where there is time to develop a story.

However, most metaphor has to work, in contemporary poems, within a far more limited compass. And very often it is far less obvious than the Arnold example. If it is 'good' metaphor, it will have a powerful effect, even if there may be a kind of mysterious quality about it.

Metaphor can do what other devices of language can't do.

Of course, you may disagree with the choice of any one particular example, but here are some that strike me as particularly effective:

'Then is my daily life a narrow room' (E. St. Vincent Millay).

'The goat, with amber dumb-bells in his eyes' (N. MacCaig).
'The wind flung a magpie away and a black
Black gull bent like an iron bar slowly' (Ted Hughes).
'He was my North, my South, my East and West,
My working week and my Sunday rest,
My noon, my midnight, my talk, my song;
I thought that love would last for ever: I was wrong' (W. H. Auden).

I hesitate even to quote the above examples of metaphorical usage, never mind supply more, because there is one impression I emphatically don't want to give.

It's this: metaphor isn't some trick that can be learned, then 'applied', the way you can deliberately use alliteration, or calculate a specific rhythmical effect, or adopt a set stanza-form/rhyme-scheme.

In fact, I believe that exactly the wrong way to go about it is to 'plan' a poem, then have in mind the idea of adding metaphors, as if you stuck them on a poem like flavours on a cake. That would be disastrous. They wouldn't grow from the poetic impulse, and wouldn't belong in any inherent sense to what you have to say.

In other words, I don't think I can give practical hints about using metaphor the way I have been able to give fairly practical advice on other aspects of the poet's craft.

So what is the point of going into the matter of metaphor at all?

I think what can happen is this: If you are aware of metaphor, and pay concentrated attention to the way that good poets use metaphor, as you write your own pieces it will be more likely that any potential for metaphorical expression will be encouraged. You should recognise when metaphors you use are tired, dead, cliché-ridden, and when, on the other hand, you have coined a metaphor that is appropriate, powerful, expressive.

I think that the test of a metaphor is that it is striking, appropriate, and not strained. It should express what you want to say better than any other words could, and have an impact greater than a plain literal statement.

It may be that you write in a style that employs metaphor very little, which is quite possible. If you do, don't try to tart it up (a metaphor) with extraneous metaphorical expressions.

But remember that poets for centuries have been availing themselves of the force that lies in figurative language, so it's foolish to ignore the possibilities.

If you do employ figurative language effectively in your work, your poetry is much more likely to burn into the reader's consciousness.

Metaphorically speaking.

Jim McIntosh has two booklets on poetry published by Dundee College of Education and a chapter in the Dundee Book. *He has written articles, reviews and poems for a wide variety of publications – from the* Guardian *to* Mother and Baby, *from* France *to* Annabel, *and from the* Scotsman *to* Topical Books.

Strictures on Structure

Jim McIntosh

He was an only child, and it was wartime. These weren't the days when television was available for an ordinary family. Radio perhaps, but TV – no. However, one way to pass the time was to scribble, to tell stories, to use your imagination.

And when the motivation included prizes offered by a national newspaper, and even more, publication of the stories (the kind that began with words supplied by the paper, the story needing to be completed), then writing poured out.

At that time, the boy who wrote didn't know he was one day to be a successful writer, a writer of poetry, short stories, thrillers, and historical romances, someone in demand at Writers' Conferences, someone whose books supply colour, excitement and romance to countless readers.

Once he gained confidence, his career developed. He worked (not unexpectedly) in a bookshop, but soon he was writing more seriously. And the market that beckoned at first was the American market . . .

That's one way to begin an article, in this case a profile of a writer. It's probably the simplest way, the chronological approach, starting at the beginning, developing through the middle, reaching the end.

You don't have to start from the womb (nor continue to the tomb), but the general approach is one that follows a clear line of development, earlier to later, the guidelines being the events of the subject's life.

But you are free, of course, to present the material in a catchy way, and to give some details to establish a context (eg here, the different conditions in the boy's youth, compared with now). And you have to consider the use of a style that might help to offset the slightly predictable approach of the article.

Here the style includes the structure of the opening sentence, using a rhythm and vocabulary reminiscent of 'he was her only son, and she was a widow', from the Bible. And you can, of course, 'flashforward' now and again, as here, where his bright future is suggested. But you don't want to give too much away, so keep that device to a minimum.

* * *

For the first time, one of Jessica Stirling's novels is to be serialised in a national women's magazine. With every title, the number of sales increases and increases.

Jessica Stirling (in reality, Hugh C. Rae, a Scottish writer who originally made his name mainly with thrillers) has had to cut down on some of 'her' other activities, such as teaching creative writing, and has now had to succumb at last to modern technology, namely the word-processor.

Success means a whirlwind of activities, more and more invitations to speak, more tyro writers seeking help and encouragement, more conference organisers sending hopeful letters to elicit personal appearances. As I sit talking with him, Hugh speaks entertainingly and informatively about the writing game, and he speaks with the wisdom and authority that wide experience confers.

This is a far cry from the only child in wartime, alleviating his aloneness and exercising his imagination by scribbling entries to newspaper writing-competitions, and gradually having it dawn upon him that he wanted to be a writer.

He says now that he would still write, even if he didn't have to write in order to earn a living. He is in the position of a climber reaching the difficult summit, who can look back on a long, rocky path, and note the milestones and landmarks that indicate progress.

What have these been?

This is another approach, made familiar through countless films and TV dramas: the flashback. Here, you start with the subject in the present, economically safe, even perhaps fabulously wealthy, coping with the stresses of an achieved success, possibly with new problems.

How far you flash back is up to you. Obviously if you go right back ('little did Mrs Rae know, when her eight-pound baby was born in Upperhill Maternity Hospital, in September 1934, that the baby now screaming in his cot would one day be the best-selling novelist . . .'), you will in effect be turning the rest of the piece into a chronological-type article, except that there is a kind of prelude added before the chronology begins.

That could be perfectly acceptable, and occurs often in interviews, as with a recent interview with Clint Eastwood in an *Independent* colour supplement, where we were given a picture of Eastwood as he is now, then the article jumped back and dealt with highlights of his career from its earliest days.

However, it is probably preferable if you jump back to the beginning, especially if there is a strong contrast (such as poverty/riches, or rejection/adulation) between the distant past and the present. This ensures that the rest of the article every now and again comes back to the present, to make various points, rather than just having a straight run from the beginning to the present day.

In this way, you might begin with the author, today, being presented with the Booker prize, then jump back to when he first had an article published (in the school magazine). You could then come back to the present to ask if he remembers that event, then take the reader back to when the budding novelist sent his first manuscript in to be reviewed, with a cheeky letter of self-promotion attached.

And so, you would move back and forward over his career, giving you a chance to make your own points and allowing you to bring in the writer's own comments on his past.

Obviously, the danger of this approach is that unless you have tight control and can write clearly, then the reader can end up confused. It's obviously a more demanding method than the chronological one. On the other hand, it's considerably more enjoyable to read.

* * *

'I was reading a History of Kilmarnock, and there was an incident there that was just unbelievable . . . the whole thing was outlined, with dates, names, number of deaths . . . you couldn't miss the drama, and all I had to do was . . .'

As he speaks, I realise I'm in the presence of a phenomenon I always welcome and treasure – an enthusiast. All the signs are there: the glowing eyes, the eloquent words, the conviction that the listener will be equally enthralled, the attention to the subject, the single-minded concentration.

Hugh Rae is an enthusiast, not to mention a witty conversationalist, and an outstanding teacher. But these are incidental. Above all, he is a writer. And a writer he has been since he whiled away the lonely hours as a schoolboy during the Second World War, sending his stories off to a national newspaper, winning prizes; then, as he got older, writing poetry and also stories for the American market.

That enthusiasm sustained him through the early days. It accompanied and inspired him when he used to get requests for 'a John O'Hara', from the editor of one of the American 'second-grade glossies' – meaning a story in the style of John O'Hara, for one of the American magazines that were just under the 'top' glossies such as Esquire *and* The New Yorker.

Obviously, to write in order to satisfy such a request (eg 'a John O'Hara') the writer had to have read John O'Hara (or Steinbeck, or Hemingway, or Fitzgerald), never mind being able to turn out a story resembling theirs; and again, enthusiasm is in evidence, enthusiasm for reading, for literature in general, for analysing writers' style, for practising the craft . . .

Here is a third approach: taking a striking characteristic (or perhaps characteristics) of the subject, and writing the article from that point.

What are the problems here? Well, the first one is that you have to find a characteristic in your subject that will genuinely bind the whole thing together, not just some flimsy, dreamed-up gimmick. If you can find it, then you present the subject more in a series of vignettes, rather than in a chronological or flashback-plus-chronological style.

This approach is less likely to give a vast number of facts, and the reader won't have such a comprehensive view of the person being profiled. But what they may well have is a more striking and human picture, a sense of the person's personality, possibly a more memorable impression of him.

Inherent in this is another possible risk: the result will seem itsy-bitsy, fragmented.

However, that can be avoided, if you genuinely give a great deal of thought to finding the pivotal characteristic in the first place, and if you make sure that you range over the person's life/personality in a wide enough way.

Given the limitations of space, I'll try out the third method a little further here, since it is the most difficult, and try to furnish more information about Hugh Rae, through the 'outstanding characteristic' method. You might continue like this (from example three, above) perhaps.

When he was approached, some years ago, by a publisher wishing to fill a recent 'blank' in their lists, Hugh hesitated at first, since what was wanted was a historical romance told from the woman's perspective. He could easily have said that his writing till then had been firmly based in the world of the thriller: he had dealt in violence, aggression, the denizens of the 'mean streets'. He had no experience of telling stories from the woman's point of view.

But he was a writer, a professional, eager and enthusiastic about exploring the further reaches of the craft. So what did he do?

He teamed up with Peggy Coughlin, an experienced serial writer, and between them they created 'Jessica Stirling'. This writing of historical novels also necessitated delving into a vast number of books, records, archives, memoirs, accounts of trades and professions . . .

But books were a passion with Hugh, witness the rooms of his house groaning under the weight of thousands of volumes, and the attic of a neighbouring shop, rented out to hold even more books.

With typical concentration and thoroughness, he tackled the challenge.

And today, although he now writes the books as a solo performance, Jessica Stirling's sales are shooting higher and higher. Jessica Stirling is more and more in demand . . .

You get the general idea. Needless to say, whatever approach you try, it will be based on the same foundation: the *collection* of all the relevant facts, the *selection* of what will make the most interesting article, and then the *organising* of the material according to the method you decide to adopt.

It's also the case that although I have divided the approaches into three, as you become more experienced, you may well find that you can combine these in different ways, eg the straight chronological can allow for the characteristic method within its confines.

Why not select a subject, do the research, then try the three methods one after the other? Practice will help you become more skilled.

No one ever promised you'd learn to write in a short time. Just as well.

5

A WRITER'S LIFE AND BUSINESS

The beginning writer may think of writing as an art form and wait for the muse to inspire his or her masterpiece. The successful writer knows that writing is more of a craft than an art – and that the actual writing is merely a part of the *business*.

The beginner waits hopefully, for inspiration to strike. The successful writer *arranges* to be inspired – daily.

A successful writer has to be *organised*. A working schedule – when and where you are going to do your writing – has to be established; information – some call it research – has to be collected; and then there has to be a system for the filing/storage of this collected information – to ensure ready retrieval.

Both before and after the actual writing, it is wise to consider who is going to buy it: if you can't find an editor or publisher to accept your work, it's unlikely to get read – and writing which is not read is incomplete communication. The successful writer is the writer who thinks about selling his/her work.

Some of the business and organisational aspects of the writer's life have slipped into earlier sections of this book – notably Marian Hardless's 'Twenty Tips' in the non-fiction section. And I suppose my own piece about 'Selling a Non-Fiction Book' is also more than a little business oriented.

In this section though, I have brought together a number of more specific 'Life and Business' pieces: one-time editor Martin Horan reminds us of the writer's basic 'facts of life', pointing out that 'The Editor's Always Right!'; Jim Rees looks at and advises on the sources, collection methods and organisation of the ever-essential 'Research for Writers'; Elizabeth Balfour emphasises – if emphasis is necessary – the importance of 'Marketing Matters'; and clergyman's wife Brenda Courtie offers a lot of practical advice on 'How To Market Your Books by Guest Speaking'. Don't think that once your book is published it's then all up to the publisher; the successful author is the one who also helps with the selling process. Brenda's article tells you how.

The Editor's Always Right!

Martin Horan

Fed up of not getting the breaks? Ever feel junk gets published while your best work earns rejection slips? Are you positive your writing's excellent but, due to the countless rejection slips, you're beginning to lose faith in your abilities?

Having edited a newspaper and co-edited two literary magazines, I can assure you most editors aren't cold-hearted monsters. They're on the lookout for new writers. Especially if they show promise. And they really know who does, believe me.

Just about all writers, sometime during their career, go through those feelings I mentioned. We all get despondent – and blame it on everything but ourselves. Usually, the editor gets it first!

If you're not getting published the fault lies with you. Ouch. *That* sounds pretty cold-hearted. Maybe. But whenever an MS is returned, 99 times out of a 100, it's the writer's fault.

Sure, I can blame all the editors so you'll think I'm a swell bloke. That's great. But it won't help you to get into print.

Admittedly, there's always the one chance in a hundred where it *is* the editor's fault. If that's the case with you then you don't have to worry. Most editors know their business. If you're doing everything right, you'll soon be in print.

My advice as a former editor – as well as a frequently published writer – is take it that **you** are in the wrong, *never* the editor. Even if you are a literary genius, that attitude will only increase your value as a writer.

If you're convinced you are perfect, you won't progress. You won't think you'll have to. By that attitude you won't be able to! Nor will you be able to get into print.

You must be objective regarding your work. Scrutinise it meticulously. You cannot rectify a wrong until or unless you see that wrong. Look for what you're doing wrong. When you see it, admit it.

And you can't stop there. You must change. It's no use seeing where you're going wrong and then carrying on doing wrong.

Sounds obvious? Then you'd be surprised by the mountains of contributions editors receive that are badly laid out. Or have bad grammar or spelling.

Why?

Because the writers are convinced their 'work' is so good they don't need to bother about these things. *As long as you ignore these things you will* NEVER – EVER – *get your work published.* Not by any reputable newspapers, magazines, or journals, you won't.

Think I kid? Then you just carry on regardless and you'll find out – the hard way.

But maybe you think you're the exception to the rule – as many writers, to the result of piles of rejection slips, do – and so editors will treat your work as a special case? What I'd like to know is: why should they?

Because you're a genius! Now why didn't I think of that?

Your short stories are much better than Maupassant's. Your novels say much more than Tolstoy's. As a journalist neither Conor Cruise O'Brien nor Peregrine Worsthorne can hold a candle to you. Essays? Why, Pliny the Younger, Montaigne and Charles Lamb don't have a look in.

Tell me, then, if you're so brilliant, why aren't you in print?

It would seem your literary prowess is being ignored. So why? Could it be because of your grammar, layout or spelling? You can bet your sweet typewriter on it.

I assure you editors will reject your work at a glance if your approach to these things is one of indifference. It shows. Clearly. An editor will reject a contribution at a glance because of *one* of these things. As for two, he'll be convinced you're not worth publishing. All three and he'll be convinced you're not worth even *reading*!

Are editors fools then, rejecting literary merit on superficialities? It's irrelevant. Because it doesn't alter the fact of how they operate – even supposing you were in the right and they wrong.

They have the power. You don't. They'll never change to suit you. You may as well change to suit them. You'll have to, to appear in print. You won't if you don't.

Does that sound like rough justice? I'm sure it does. I'm sure it also sounds a bit oversimplified to you. But I'm trying to make a point. Very strongly. You'll get nowhere till you satisfy the editor.

It's silly to think you're the exception to the rule. Many writers who aren't getting the breaks think exactly that. The reason the greats and the famous are in print is because they took the steps to ensure they pleased their editors/publishers. Take a tip from them if you won't from me.

If you're still not convinced, then you do have to admit that good writing often doesn't get published just due to bad timing or marketing. For starters, you surely believe that of your own work. So if that's the case, doesn't it stand to reason that good writing will be rejected for the other reasons I've given?

The 'image' of the writer is popularly portrayed as that of the rebel or non-conformist. Some like to live up to that image and think submitting shoddy MSS does so. But a writer's image has nothing to do with his output and a lot to do with fashion. Great writers are never slaves of fashion. If you don't know that, editors do.

I read an article encouraging writers. It mentioned that masterpieces have been written in pencil on scraps of paper. And so they have. But we have to watch such 'encouragement' because it usually gives the wrong impression.

Beginners think they can do it. And they should. A writer should write with whatever comes to his hand – to *begin*. The purpose is to get started at all costs. But it's not how you conclude. The writers who wrote such masterpieces didn't send them to publishers like that.

Robert Tressel's book *The Ragged-Trousered Philanthropists* was rejected because it was hand-written. It wasn't published till long after his death soon after his daughter paid to have it typed out. It's now a famous book.

In certain cases, such as *Papillon*, where the author was incarcerated and then a fugitive, hand-written MSS are acceptable. Because the publisher knows it will add to the chances of selling such a book. But that's the exception – and a very rare exception.

But, honestly, would it do that for your writing? Would it make it more saleable?

Even Solzhenitsyn, who wrote much of his work in prison or confinement, and under the close scrutiny of tyrants, made sure his submitted work was done so in the highest professional manner. But Solzhenitsyn isn't a literary great for nothing.

First impressions count in the world at large – in every walk of life. So it's natural they count in the writing field. If you give an editor a bad first impression, it could be difficult trying to rectify it in the future.

I cannot emphasise these things too strongly. They do matter. If your work isn't getting published are you sure these aren't some of the reasons? In my experience I've found the reasons mentioned here are among the main ones for rejection slips.

True, your work can be rejected for other valid reasons but the instances given here are prerequisites for publication. You can have your work rejected for being the wrong length or the wrong subject. But the correct length and correct subject won't get you published unless your MS is submitted properly. Properly means with correct grammar and spelling.

It also means being double-spaced, numbered correctly, titled correctly and with all the other essential information on the title page.

Whatever the reason your work's being rejected, the fault is yours. Even if your layout's spot on and your grammar and spelling are immaculate, you must ask yourself, 'What am I doing wrong?'

I made the same mistakes in the past. I paid for them with rejections. I learnt my lesson. *Then* my work appeared in print. So write, getting it right who's right. That's the editor – *always*.

Martin Horan has been a small publisher, an editor (and co-editor) and a columnist. He is now a freelance writer – and has written short stories, articles and poems for a variety of publications. He has written a number of successful non-fiction books, mainly about Scotland; he has also produced a book of cartoons and funny poems in Scots dialect. He is now searching for a publisher for a comic novel.

Research for Writers

Jim Rees

What is your first duty as a journalist? To inform the readers, I hear you reply. Fine, but where do you get your information?

Every good newspaper and magazine has its library containing not only a wide range of reference books but also thousands – perhaps even millions – of press cuttings filed under specific headings. When a news story breaks, these files are referred to for background information.

If you are a freelance journalist your office (which could be a corner of your bedroom, attic or garden shed) should have such an archive.

That doesn't mean you have to have the most up-to-date set of encyclopaedia on the market. Your local library will have most of the expensive reference books you require. Use them. The library service is something no journalist can afford to overlook.

Nevertheless, you should have a reasonably good library of your own. A good dictionary, thesaurus and a few general reference volumes are adequate to begin with. Your choice of reference books will, of course, depend a great deal on what you want to write about.

One book all writers should have is the *Writers' & Artists' Yearbook* which includes a list of books to help your writing.

Books can be expensive, so you should concentrate on accumulating your own cuttings library. That may seem a daunting task, but it's quite simple and once you've begun you'll be surprised how quickly such an archive grows – and your only outlay is for brown A4 size envelopes and cardboard boxes.

So, how do you begin?

Press cuttings:
As ever, start with what you know. Your personal likes and dislikes will determine the type of information you should collect.

Let's say you're a keen philatelist. You probably buy one or two magazines catering for the hobby on a regular basis. Understandably, you would prefer to leave magazines intact rather than mutilate them for your cuttings files. Leave them intact, although it might make locating a particular piece a little more difficult.

Articles about stamps, postal services, postmarks and off-beat pieces such as 'Letter Takes 85 Years to Reach Destination' appear in all sorts of publications. These are the stuff of cuttings files.

Always be on the look out for cuttings. Ask your relatives and friends to save their old newspapers and magazines for you. The next time you see a discarded publication on a bus, train, or park bench scan it. You never know what you'll find.

Even if your field of interest is relatively narrow at first you'll be amazed how quickly your store of information will build up. After a while you'll discover you are digressing into other areas and as your collection grows so will your range of interests.

My cuttings library began with anniversary articles. I had three brown envelopes. One each for Christmas, Easter and Halloween. Within a year Christmas had five envelopes – Santa Claus, birds and beasts associated with Christmas, Christmas music, events on Christmas Day in the past, and Christmas cards and customs.

I now have many more.

The Easter file, too, became bulky and diverse in a short time. It has since been subdivided into customs, Easter abroad, and events at Eastertide in times past.

Not only had my three original files to be subdivided but over the past six years my cuttings library has swelled to cover almost 200 themes. In an article such as this it would be impossible – and unnecessary – to list them all, but the following should give some idea how the library developed.

Anniversaries – subdivided into:
New Year and Calendar pieces;
Candlemas;
St Valentine's Day;
Leap Year;
St Patrick's Day;
Grand National;
April Fools' Day;
Easter (subdivided as above);

   Halloween; and
   Christmas (subdivided as above)
American Indians
Copyright
Off-beat Crime & Punishment
Duelling
Explorers – subdivided into:
   geographical locations
Famous Figures – subdivided into:
   showbiz;
   artists & composers;
   sporting personalities;
   philanthropists;
   writers;
   colourful characters;
   politicians;
   heads of state and revolutionaries;
   scientists
Maritime History – subdivided into:
   marine art;
   shipwrecks;
   sea mysteries;
   rescues;
   historic ships;
   marine archaeology;
   customs & beliefs of seafarers through the centuries
Quests for Lost Treasure
Time Capsules
Wills

Some of these themes overlap. Quests For Lost Treasure and Shipwrecks are obvious examples. If I am writing an article about treasure seekers in general I consult both files. Likewise, reports of the excavation of the Tudor ship *Mary Rose* could be filed under Historic Ships or Time Capsules.

Get the picture?

The larger your collection grows the more important it becomes to keep it tidy and well catalogued. Never be reluctant to create a new file or subdivision.

The purpose of any filing system is to facilitate retrieval of information as quickly as possible and with the minimum of fuss.

If I hadn't subdivided the Christmas file whenever I deemed necessary you can imagine the trouble I would now have in locating a particular snippet among several hundred.

This article is, in the main, aimed at writers of journalism, but fiction writers should also have a cuttings library. The content may differ but the system is the same. Fiction writers should keep cuttings of bizarre situations, characters, crime, etc, which they can twist to their own requirements.

Although the bulk of my writing is factual, I have had several short stories published. In three of those stories I used the same key character and he has developed into a fuller 'person' with each story. When I come across a piece in a newspaper I think would suit my character I cut it out and file it under the heading 'Situations for Declan'.

I now have over 20 snippets which I hope to use when time allows.

Press and public relations officers
While your cuttings library is indispensable it will seldom give you all the information you require.

For example, a few cuttings in my Santa Claus file concern children's rather mercenary letters to the poor soul who spends 364 days a year alone and unwanted at the North Pole. I wondered how the Post Office deals with such letters.

As all my Christmas cuttings are at least a year old, I needed more recent information. I wrote to the Press Officer in the General Post Office. Within days I received a detailed reply and suitable photographs to illustrate the article.

Most government offices and services have Press and Public Relations Officers who are delighted to help the freelance.

Commercial concerns are equally anxious to have articles about themselves published in newspapers and magazines. Within the past few months I received publicity photographs from a fireworks manufacturer to illustrate a Guy Fawkes article.

The company's name doesn't even appear in the article, but the photographs are indirect advertisements for fireworks and the company concerned is satisfied with that – and so they should be. If they were to take out an advertisement in the usual way it would cost several thousands of pounds. This way it costs a couple of photographs.

It is a mutually beneficial exercise and you should never feel you are asking for a hand-out when you write to a Press Officer for information or illustrations.

When requesting information keep your letter brief and to the point. Include details of what you're writing about and for whom you are writing.

Many writers starting their careers are reluctant to say they are writing for a particular publication until they have made the sale. This should not be the case. If you have a publication in mind and you intend to write the article to suit you are quite entitled to say that you are writing for that publication.

I usually enclose a short list of questions (never more than ten) which require brief answers and I have seldom been disappointed with the response.

The Royal National Lifeboat Institution, The Blood Transfusion Service, numerous libraries, museums and tourist boards are among the many bodies who have helped me.

Once you have made contact with a Press Officer ask that your name be added to their mailing list for press releases. I have sold quite a few articles written from press releases I would not have received had my name not been on the company's mailing list.

When you get the information you've requested write a note of thanks. It is merely common courtesy – and it helps to cement your relationship with the supplier of the information.

Who to contact and where

I have already referred to the *Writers' & Artists' Yearbook*. It contains a list of government offices and public services complete with addresses. However, contact names are not included, but in most cases letters addressed to the Press Officer or Public Relations Officer will suffice.

Finding appropriate addresses in the private sector is equally straightforward. The telephone directory, particularly the classified directory, should not be overlooked.

For example, let's return to the Guy Fawkes article.

I had no idea where to get suitable illustrations. I, therefore, used the following sequence of thought. Guy Fawkes – November 5 – fireworks – manufacturers – telephone directory.

I wrote to the Press Officer of the first firework manufacturers listed and bingo! It really is as simple as that.

I could have approached one of the many excellent picture libraries (again, listed in *W&A Yearbook*), but in my experience the fees charged for publication rights often outweigh the benefits.

Embassies and Consulates

So far I have dealt with gathering information within national boundaries, but if you need information from abroad the telephone directory, classified or otherwise, is of little use.

Embassies and Diplomatic Consulates are always willing to answer enquiries concerning their countries and cultures.

I was once writing an article about a major exhibition in Legoland A/S in Denmark. I had no idea what part of Denmark Legoland was in so I contacted the Press Officer of the Danish Embassy and was quickly given the exact address.

I then wrote to the company P.R.O. who supplied me with more photographs than I could use in one article – so I wrote several. Also included were a booklet on the exhibition I was researching, a booklet on other collections in the complex and a booklet about Legoland in general.

That's how it's done.

Personal contacts

An address book is an important part of the freelance's tool-kit. When you make contact with a Press Officer, company P.R.O., or even an interesting character in the local pub, enter his or her name in your address book.

Many entries in my address book are classified in the same manner as a classified telephone directory. Under A is archaeology and the name, address and phone number of an archaeologist who has helped me in the past. Under S (for stamps) is the name of a philatelist friend and a scuba-diving contact.

It's all very simple – and that's the secret. Keep it simple.

Gathering information may seem an insurmountable problem, but the more you do it the more confident and competent you become. Each time you gather information through personal contact you achieve two goals in one exercise. You add to your data files and to your list of contacts.

Now, start building your library. Below are three books which will repay your investment many times over.
1. *Writers' & Artists' Yearbook*, publ. by A&C Black, London, £5.95.
2. *Research for Writers*, 3rd edition, publ. by Black, written by Ann Hoffmann. £6.95.
3. *The Cambridge University Guide to the Museums of Britain and Ireland* by Kenneth Hudson & Ann Nichols, publ. by Cambridge University Press. £15.00.

Jim Rees has written hundreds of articles and stories which have been published in Ireland, Britain, America, Norway and Denmark. He also writes a monthly and a quarterly column. He has written one book on the ships of the schooner port of Arklow, Ireland, and is near to completing a biography of the sea captain, Robert Halpin.

Marketing Matters

Elizabeth Balfour

Marketing? When you hear the word do you mentally turn to another channel or even switch off completely? It's understandable – inflationary spiral . . . socio-economic mix . . . mechanistic organisation . . . psychographics – with jargon like this, who needs it?

Yet marketing is something we all do with our work at some time or another, whether we write for pleasure, for profit, or for both.

Marketing is defined as 'the management process responsible for identifying, anticipating and satisfying customer requirements profitably' by the Chartered Institute of Marketing.

Let's deal with the first and the last phrase together. The writer is generally his/her own manager – after all, we choose our own hours and methods of work, we must be 'self-starters', we have our own reasons for writing.

Profit in this case cannot be reduced to financial gain – for most of us this will be limited in any case – but must surely include the sheer pleasure of sharing our work with others. Think of chuckles of laughter at a funny piece in a poetry reading; the round of applause for a short story delivered at a workshop; the pride in seeing your own name in print in the local newspaper or your favourite magazine; the novel on sale at last.

Identify, anticipate and satisfy. These are processes we follow unconsciously, but which often lead us down dark alleyways when it comes to presenting or selling our work.

Identify the customer's requirements; this is vital. I once sat through a long poem at a 'Poems and Pints' session. Frankly no one wanted to listen to a clever, complex, intellectual 20 minutes' worth after a few beers on a Friday night. It may have been excellent stuff, but we were all relieved when someone coughed loudly and reminded the poetess that her time was up. She had put her own need to read this poem before the requirements of her audience.

My favourite piece, heard at the same venue but on another occasion, was a letter allegedly written by one of Robert Burns' girlfriends from her bed in the Venereal Diseases Clinic of the local hospital. It was funny, vulgar, unusual, unexpected and, on St Valentine's Day, a timely antidote to too much romance. (Also a fair reflection on Rabbie Burns, very much the macho hero in my home, Scotland.) The (true) author didn't particularly like it, but, egged on by his local Writer's Circle, he added it, successfully, to his contribution for the evening.

Identification of customer requirements means something no writer can do without: market research. As they say in the army, 'Time spent in reconnaissance is never wasted.' It is something on which big companies spend small fortunes, the lifeblood of politicians and pundits. For writers it involves simply reading and asking.

Whatever you are working on – it has been done before. If you are part of a writers' workshop planning to self publish your work, look at how other workshops have done this. Ask what their most popular poems have been – did they fare better with short stories or poems, humorous or serious items? What kind of a balance is there? Read through their publications and see which you as a group enjoy. Count the words of your favoured pieces – look at the style, the content. Learn from the success and failure of others.

If you write short stories, which are always difficult to place, pore through all the magazines which use them. Again, count the number of words, look at the themes, look at the kinds of hero/heroine, the locations used, and so on. I love short stories and feel myself that there could be a revival of this medium soon. To this day I believe that reading Damon Runyan's wonderful stories in *Guys and Dolls* while in labour ensured that I had an easy delivery and bore a child with an excellent sense of humour.

I have tried hard to sell my own stories, but have come to the conclusion that the world is just not ready for them, yet, after all, Van Gogh never sold a painting in his lifetime. Market research has proved to me that there is no requirement for my stories, so at least I know that if I write them it is simply for my own pleasure.

Article writing is a very wide field in terms of consumer requirement. Besides local and national newspapers, there are magazines on everything from accountancy to yachting, and surely most writers could earn an honest coin or two here, as well as gaining valuable experience and prestige.

In a weighty publication known as *JICNARS* (Joint Industry Committee for National Readership Surveys), you can find detailed analysis of the readership of a wide range of publications, discovering, if you wish, the age range, TV viewing habits and social status of your targeted magazine's readers.

If this proves heavy going careful study of the small ads will give a good indication of the nature of the readership.

My own market research is sometimes sparked off in unorthodox ways. Recently I found myself elbowed aside while browsing at our biggest bookstore by hunky Rohan types reaching for the outdoor magazines. It occurred to me that I could write up a (totally rainsodden) hillwalk I had undertaken as part of some historical research. After all, these people looked as if they lived in waterproof clothing.

I went to the library and perused all the back copies of the walking and climbing magazines, and sent off a few letters outlining my suggestion. I had one encouraging reply and decided to phone the editor to ask how many words he needed. It turned out that he was really looking for short items rather than any more – as he put it – 'turn left at the stile' articles. I came up with several brief ideas, which he liked. Last week I pushed past the rucksacks and found one of my own small pieces in print.

If it comes to writing something longer – children's books, the novel or the informative book – research is even more important. Really look at what people buy and at what people borrow from the library. How many words do they read, what genre is most popular, what are the heroes and heroines like, do the kind of stories you want to write match those which people want to read?

Children are highly critical, and always seem to love tales of horror and hardship. Your local librarian will know exactly what they borrow, if not why.

Publishers are inundated daily by unsuitable MSS, but it is quite possible to find out what they are likely to consider, by looking at what they produce. Books like the annual *The Writer's Handbook* are invaluable. Why not search through libraries and bookshops until you become familiar with the names of those publishing in your particular genre?

If you can identify your customers' requirements you are more than halfway to success in writing.

Anticipation is the next aspect of marketing. Beatrix Potter, turned down by every publisher, knew there was a need for books which were, for one thing, small enough for children to hold in their hands. So she began by self publishing. Remember that she had already done a good deal of market research by writing, giving and reading her own work to her small friends. Her work has since given pleasure to generations of children.

It's often possible to predict what will be 'flavour of the month' in your own field of work or interest and get in first with some relevant information. There is a great trade in 'anniversary' articles, and it's easy enough to find out who was born/married/died, what battles were fought, what important events took place in any month or year through your library – and link them with your writing. Then there is the whole area of seasonal items. 'Be topical and timely' as I was once advised, and you will go far in anticipating your readers' needs.

Marketing also involves presentation. Most people have access to a typewriter or word processor, and the chance to learn how to use it. If not there are office service firms who will type out anything handwritten, so there can be no excuse for poorly presented work.

Don't forget there are correspondence and evening classes on offer, as well as plenty of 'How to' books, for those of you who want to know more about successful writing. Writers' workshops are invaluable for offering the opportunity to learn about your work from the reactions of other people. Personally, I have always treasured the advice not to try out work on close family or friends.

Publicity is another part of marketing – look how many books are sold in association with TV serials and, for that matter, how many celebrities turn up on the chat shows with a copy of their latest book under their arm. While not everyone would like to be associated with so much hype, a modest review in a local or community paper, or a slot on local radio, can be helpful publicity for anyone. You have to let your customers know you're there.

I was introduced to the concept of marketing on a Business Start Up Course, which at first seemed to have nothing to do with writing. I've since discovered that it is not enough to want to write, or even to write well. By using marketing principles I've learned to be more objective and to find a place for my work. It has been hard, and I have been disappointed to discover how much compromise is needed for any progress.

Even so, there is not much in this world that can beat the thrill of turning a printed page and finding your own name at the foot of it.

Elizabeth Balfour, having succeeded in selling a number of articles in her spare time, gave up work, took the 'Enterprise Allowance', and now writes full time. She has now sold more of her writing and hopes to get a 'trail' book published.

How to Market Your Books by Guest Speaking

Brenda Courtie

Have you noticed what happens at a party when it comes out in conversation that you're a writer?

Readers of *Writers' Monthly* know, of course, that writers are dedicated craftsmen exercising well-honed skills, but the rest of the world tends to be a little awed by us. Tell them you're a teacher or a van-driver and you'll get a polite nod. Tell them you're a writer and they do a double take.

You may only have published one short story, an even shorter article and a handful of knitting hints, but call yourself a writer and the world invests you with sudden glamour.

It's irrational. It may even be irresponsible. But it's a fact. More than that, if you need one, it's a marketing opportunity. Because if you're prepared to exploit the cachet of 'being a writer', there are people out there who will queue up to come and see a real live specimen, hear you speak about your craft and, hopefully, buy your books.

I have an arrangement with my publisher whereby I can have books to sell myself, so that, when I accept an invitation to be a guest-speaker at a meeting or dinner, I take a box of books along with me.

You could arrange for the local bookshop to deal with the selling. But even if you don't have books for sale at the event itself, guest-speaking is still a marketing opportunity because what you are selling in either case is not your books, but yourself.

Once those people out there feel they know you personally, and like you, they'll want to buy your books. Buying a book by an author they've met is all part of the glamour.

However, writing and speaking about writing are different things. Some writers may feel nervous and ill-equipped at the thought of becoming a guest speaker. So I've put together some tips on public speaking, based on my own experience, under three headings:

- On your phone
- In your file
- On your feet

On your phone

The more you know about a speaking engagement in advance, the better prepared you can be and the more relaxed on the actual occasion. And most of this information comes to me via telephone conversations with the 'speaker secretary' of whichever group is inviting me to speak to them. When the secretary phones, make sure you ask these questions:

Who is the audience? – Women's Institute? Rotary Club? Steelworkers' Poetry Workshop? Obviously, the *content* of your talk will vary according to who'll be hearing it. I have to be a bit careful about this, because I have several 'speaking hats' as a freelance writer, clergy-wife and adult education tutor.

How many? – Is this a regular weekly meeting of ten folk, or a huge annual rally of 2,000? The *style* of your talk will vary according to the dynamics of the meeting. A homely chat will suit the Ladies' Afternoon Guild, but a prestigious Media and Communications Conference, for example, would require a more formal informative lecture.

Venue? – Will you need a map? Will they provide a display table? Does it need/have P.A.?

Time? – Not just day and hour, but the running order of the programme. At what point in the meeting do you come on? After the business? After the meal? Before the tea and biscuits? And for how long will you be expected to speak? Make them be specific about this, then practise your talk *to the minute*. You won't sell anything if you overrun and they're all dying to leave to catch the train or go to the loo.

Is there a fee? – Amounts vary, according to which league you're in. Church and charity groups will probably be able to offer expenses only. But Women's Institutes, Townswomen's Guilds, Businessmen's/women's groups and Luncheon Clubs all expect to pay their speakers. £20 is fair for a new speaker. Excellent entertainers who are in great demand but not in the 'household name' bracket can expect between £40 and £60. Some Arts Associations award grants to writers' groups as a percentage of a fee offered to a visiting writer-speaker.

When you've gathered all the advance information you can, it should go in your 'Speaking Engagements' file.

In your file
But the most important item in your file on the day is your prepared talk, which you only start putting together once you know something about the event.

Constructing a talk is akin to writing an article. You need a catchy opening, a co-ordinated middle and a punchy ending. But never forget that the overall aim is to sell your books by selling *yourself*. So tell them about yourself – how you started writing, your first big break, your usual writing routine. Tell them about the best moments and the worst. The funniest, the saddest.

Punctuate your talk with illustrations, using two kinds in particular: i) personal anecdotes (these make your audience feel they really do know you) and ii) extracts from your writing. Make these extracts topical to your talk, e.g. seasonal, or with local references, or with appropriate nostalgic references, or some fiction based on fact (which you have shared as an anecdote). It's often a good idea to finish with an extract – particularly if it's a cliff-hanger!

When you've put your talk together, practise it. Read it word for word out loud, including your selected extracts, so that you know exactly how long it is. To the minute. If they *should* stand on their seats and yell for an encore, you can always give them another extract.

Some speakers tape-record their talk at home and play it back to hear the gaffes. An even better idea is to ask a friend to listen to your talk 'in the flesh' – they'll tell you if you have any unconscious but irritating habits, like jingling the loose change in your trousers pocket.

I write out every talk I do, word for word. This is partly because I get nervous and if I just have headings I find they become totally meaningless between home and platform. And partly because if I just have headings, and I'm nervous, I talk for too long between the headings. But although my talk is typed out in full, or written out neatly on cards which I find easier to manage, I make every effort to put it over in as spontaneous a manner as possible. I practise it at home so that I'm thoroughly familiar with the text and can 'speak' it rather than 'read' it on the day.

O.K. You've sorted out the details on the phone. You've got your carefully prepared talk in your file. You're on the platform, being introduced. And now you're . . .

On your feet

Even before you say anything there are further minor preparations. Do a quick mental check on ventilation and visibility, with requests for people to open windows or move chairs if necessary.

If you don't, they'll shuffle after you've started, which can be very off-putting.

Then, before you start on the text of your rehearsed talk with its catchy opening, a further two things – i) thank the chairperson for the wonderful introduction even if it wasn't – ii) say something pleasant about the club/hall/meal/town/anything relevant. This little preamble registers two important things in the subconscious of your audience – it marks you out as a confident 'pro' rather than a nervous amateur, and it warms them towards you. And that's what you're there for – *you* sell yourself so that *they* buy your books.

Even the most experienced public speakers have felt that fleeting panic when every eye in the room is fixed on you and every ear awaits your first word. But the experienced speaker also knows that it *is* only fleeting, and that there are various tricks of the trade that will get you through your ordeal with confidence and even enjoyment.

Here, then, is a list of the most obvious tips for public speakers:

- *Dress for the occasion* – you are your own best, or worst, visual aid. ('The medium is the message'). Be smart, but not garish or too sombre. And not distractingly bitty.
- *Make friends before you speak* – try to talk to one or two individuals before the meeting starts.
- *Adopt a balanced stance* – feet about 12"–14" apart, to avoid wobbling and knee-knocking.
- *Have your script at a good height* – hold it up if there isn't a decent lectern, but don't let it hide your face.
- *Breathe deeply before you start* – to help to relax you.
- *Speak slowly* – too slowly, to your nervous ear. It won't be.

- *Speak loudly* – aim to hit the back wall.
- *Use the microphone* – if there's a microphone, there ought to be someone there on a mixing desk adjusting your sound level. A rule of thumb is to stand 12" away from the mic and still speak loudly. If it pops or howls you're too close, not too loud. Don't assume that you can use a quiet studio voice just because there's a microphone – that only works if you've got the right mic, the right P.A. equipment and the right man on the mixer.
- *Vary time and speed* – with experience (or a lot of rehearsals at home) you will find that you can create different effects with your voice by changing the speed or tone of your delivery. This is especially effective if you're reading extracts.
- *Allow for response* – if you tell a funny story, allow time for the audience to laugh. (And pray that they do!) If they should spot something funny and laugh where you weren't expecting it, pause and smile. (And ask the chairperson later what the joke was!).
- *Don't be afraid of the audience* – the chances are that few of them, if any, could do what you're doing. Keep a finger on your script to mark your place so that you can look at your audience frequently, make eye contact and smile.
- *Don't fidget* – they can usually see your feet even if you can't. (And other bits!)
- *Don't abandon your script and go on to automatic pilot* – you could be there all night. On your own.

At the end of your talk, *before* you sit down, thank your audience for being so wonderfully attentive and responsive and making your task such a pleasant one. They will love you for being so discerning about them. They will also know that you have finished and they can now clap. And rush to buy your books.

Brenda Courtie writes educational books for Lion Publishing, but has also written an autobiography, a novel and numerous articles and short stories for the religious press and the general market. She is a regular speaker at writers' groups and a popular after-dinner and luncheon speaker with a national agency.